The Microgenetic Theory of Mind and Brain

This book asks where ideas, objects and feelings come from and how they arise via an exploration of the nature of subjective experience and its relation to the world. Seeking an explanation for the experience of subjective duration and the present and in contrast to the conception of mental events as non-temporal logical solids, it explores a diachronic processual theory founded on psychological data and clinical observation that provides an explanatory "system" of thought adequate to the phenomena it is called on to explain. The author focuses on the intra-psychic sources and nature of subjective experience, with the intent of examining a variety of phenomena from the standpoint of microgenetic theory. The chapters deal with the origins of human subjectivity and the epochal nature of time and duration, change and the relevance of a theory of the mental state to dream and the waking present. Based on speculative psychology that flows from case studies in neuropsychology and concepts in process philosophy, it advances a theory of mind and brain that brings together previous, fragmentary research studies on this topic.

Jason W. Brown is a behavioural neurologist and, for over 30 years, was Clinical Professor of Neurology at New York University Medical Center, USA.

Denys Zhadiaiev is a scholar, lecturer and Associate Professor at Dnipro University of Technology, Ukraine.

Paul Stenner is Professor of Social Psychology at the Open University, UK.

The Microgenetic Theory of Mind and Brain

Selected Essays in Process Psychology

Jason W. Brown
Edited by
Denys Zhadiaiev and Paul Stenner

NEW YORK AND LONDON

First published 2025
by Routledge
605 Third Avenue, New York, NY 10158

and by Routledge
4 Park Square, Milton Park, Abingdon, Oxon, OX14 4RN

Routledge is an imprint of the Taylor & Francis Group, an informa business

ISBN: 9781032873848 (hbk)
ISBN: 9781032879970 (pbk)
ISBN: 9781003535775 (ebk)

DOI: 10.4324/9781003535775

Typeset in Times New Roman
by codeMantra

Contents

Preface

It is fair to say that much of my work has been guided by a single idea that originated in a qualitative approach to the errors that occur with focal brain damage. The account, initially of phases in language in relation to brain process, and of anatomical studies that complement the psychological model, has gradually grown to the point where the theory outstrips the data that are needed in support, which puts greater weight on the coherence of its basic assumptions. The papers in this collection represent the furthermost reach of the theory and, for now, its conceptual limit.

I am acutely aware of the theoretical nature of these chapters and the departure from many of the main lines of contemporary research. This, along with an evolutionary orientation, and an emphasis on process and continuities as opposed to logical solids, will no doubt leave some readers adrift. Hopefully, the introduction by Paul Stenner should help to locate this approach in relation to studies in both neuropsychology and process philosophy. It is my view, however, that the fate of the theory will likely require an exhaustion of the hegemony of modular thinking that has been imposed on much of philosophical psychology with the status of the theory a matter for future studies in cognition and neuroscience to resolve.

Acknowledgements

I want to express my deep gratitude for the introduction by Paul Stenner, PhD (The Open University, London, UK), to prof. dr. hab. Maria Pąchalska (Andrzej Frycz Modrzewski Krakow University, Krakow, Poland) for figures she developed for this book and for editing the manuscript and to Denys Zhadiaiev, PhD (Dnipro University of Technology, Dnipro, Ukraine).

I am also grateful to the editors of the following journals for permission to reprint articles with some revisions:

Theoretical note on the nature of the present. *Process Studies* (2018) 47 (1–2): 163–171.

Time and the dream, originally published in *Neuropsychoanalysis* (2020) 22 (1–2): 129–138.

Origins of subjective experience. *The Journal of Mind and Behavior* (2020) 41 (3 and 4): 270–279.

The Mind/Brain State. *The Journal of Mind and Behavior* (2021) 42: 1–16.

Brown, J.W., Zhadiaiev, D. From Drive to Value. *Process Studies* (2022) 51: 204–220.

Feeling and action, in press, in *Exploring Consciousness - From Non-Duality to Non-Locality*. Proceedings of conference on Consciousness. Bangalore, India, (2022).

Interviews with Jason Brown, *Mind & Matter* (2013) 11 (2): 183–203.

Jason Brown, MD
Clinical Professor, Neurology (ret)
New York University Medical Center

Introduction

Jason W. Brown - Archaeologist of Experience

Paul Stenner

Introducing Brown's 'Process Approach' to Neuropsychology

This book presents a series of papers by Jason W. Brown selected to illustrate the broad psychological and philosophical relevance of his microgenetic *process* theory of human mental functioning. Beginning with his work on the aphasias (disturbances to the formulation and understanding of language correlated with specific regional brain dysfunctions), the microgenetic theory has been developed by Brown over more than six decades. This means that the vast majority of his output has, by necessity, been excluded by the editorial process of selecting just seven papers. This editorial selection shows a preference for Brown's later work which deals with more complex and general philosophical and psychological issues like time, dream, subjectivity, value, emotion, thought and belief. This work is far upstream from the early work on aphasia, apraxia and agnosia, but it very much depends upon and develops that early work. A counter-gravitational movement from downstream to upstream might seem paradoxical, and yet, it is quite natural. Brown is not the first to have acted like the proverbial salmon swimming upstream to find its final satisfaction by revisiting its place of birth. But he is rare in so far as he recognises this inversion and makes it core to his thinking: a thinking that grasps the becoming of mental process by re-traversing it. This thinking, as we shall see, amounts to an *archaeology of experience* which effectively reverses a number of assumptions core to the long dominant paradigms of cognitive science in psychology and localisation approaches in neurology. This is important because, together, these paradigms form the pincer movement of today's cognitive neuroscience.

An 'archaeology of experience' becomes necessary once it is recognised that the progressive individuation proper to the microgenetic becoming of each and every mind/brain state or epoch re-traverses growth processes common to phylogenesis and ontogenesis, but within vastly different – yet nested – time scales: millions of years of evolution for phylogenesis; months and years of the sculpting of brain morphology for ontogenesis; and a fraction of a second for each pulse of microgenesis. In microgenesis, each mind/brain state passes,

DOI: 10.4324/9781003535775-1

in its process of actualisation, from a deep and unconscious causal vector; through the accumulation of drive and desire; to the surface of a consciously known 'object' or 'act'. In terms of the phylogenetic sequence of development (the morphology of which is laid down afresh in the ontogenesis of each individual brain), this constitutes a bottom-up passage from the archaic to the recent in evolutionary structure. Brown's microgenetic theory is a *process theory* to the extent that these three temporalities of change are not just alike but ultimately part of a unified *process.* By providing some background on Brown's work, this introduction aims to highlight a number of features of the selected material that may help the reader to consume and digest it, the better to evaluate it. I have also endeavoured to 'season' this meal with some of what has been excluded by the selection.

This introduction is structured into ten points. Sections "A Theory Grounded in Concrete Experience with the Symptoms of Brain Damage" and "The Mind/Brain State Is Not Just the Brain: Incorporating the World Itself" provide relevant background on Brown and his theory. Sections "The World Itself as the Field of Battle: The Stakes of an Adequate Theory of the Mind/Brain State", "The Front-Line Battle Is Against the Alliance of Localisation Approaches in Neuropsychology and Cognitivism" and "Revisiting the Limits of the Dominant Model of the Mind/Brain as a Machine Composed of Encapsulated Modules for Processing Information Lodged on a Circuit Board" flesh out the dominant theory Brown aims to supersede, and why it is limited. Sections "Process Philosophy as Postmodern: A Detour to Better Situate Brown's Contribution", "Continuities between Brown's Microgenetic Theory and James' Radical Empiricism" and "Microgenetic Theory as Neuropsychology in the Key of Process: Continuities with Whitehead's Philosophy of Organism" contextualise this theory in the intellectual context of 'process philosophy'. The final section "The Future of an Archaeology of Present Experience" summarises a number of significant original contributions made by Brown's application of process thought to neuropsychology.

A Theory Grounded in Concrete Experience with the Symptoms of Brain Damage

The first introductory point I wish to make is that Brown's microgenetic process theory of the mind/brain state is grounded in a thorough practical and theoretical knowledge of the impact of brain damage on mental functioning (with a particular focus on the aphasias caused by posterior and anterior lesions). This experience has provided Brown with a key to unlocking the relations between the vastly different temporalities at play in the three varieties of genesis, noted above, that are too often separated: (a) how the human brain developed through evolution (phylogenesis); (b) how it develops over the lifetime (ontogenesis) and (c) how it develops in its moment-by-moment functioning (microgenesis). It is the key – provided by this rich experience with the actual symptoms that follow from damage to different parts of the brain – that allowed Brown to practically reverse a number of assumptions long cherished amongst cognitive neuroscientists (see "The Future of an Archaeology of Present Experience" of this Introduction). This practical and theoretical experience with brain disorders in hospital settings is detailed by Pachalska (2012) and discussed in the interviews conducted with Brown by David T. Bradford in Appendix of this book. Here, I merely offer a condensed summary.

Born in 1938, Brown graduated from his premedical degree at Berkeley in 1959 inspired – amongst other things – by the evolutionary biology of Ledyard Stebbins. Four years later, he completed his medical school degree in Los Angeles, at the University of Southern California, having been influenced by Johannes Nielsen to specialise on neurology. His internship at St. Elizabeth's Hospital in Washington, D.C., in 1963 was followed by a residency at University of California, Los Angeles (UCLA) that was interrupted by the Vietnam War, for which Brown served in a Korean hospital. In 1968, he took up a post-doctoral fellowship at Boston Veteran's Hospital in Norman Geschwind's world famous Aphasia Unit. In 1970, this led to an Assistant Professorship at the Columbia-Presbyterian hospital, New York. During the mid-1970s, eager to learn from the best internationally, he worked with Henri Hecaen in Paris at the Centre Neuropsychologique et Neurolinguistique and with Anton Leischner in the Bonn aphasia laboratory. As part of a US/USSR Cultural Exchange Program, he also spent a month each with Anton Kreindler in Bucharest and with Alexander Romanovich Luria in Moscow. In 1978–79, Brown took up a Visiting Associate Professorship at the Psychology Department of Rockefeller University, funded by a grant from the National Institutes of Health. This was at the invitation of George Miller who was actively developing the field of cognitive psychology which was attracting significant funding – for conferences, seminars and new research programmes – from organisations like the Sloan Foundation. He was Clinical Professor of Neurology at New York University Medical Center from 1979 until retirement in 2006 and in 1984 started a neuropsychology laboratory in New York's Bellevue Hospital.

The Mind/Brain State Is Not Just the Brain: Incorporating the World Itself

The second introductory point I wish to make is that microgenetic theory, despite being grounded in experience with brain damage, is not just about the brain. It is about what Brown describes as *the mind/brain state* (see Chapter 2.2 of this book). It is no exaggeration to say that the question of the relation between the brain and the mind is one of the fundamental unsolved scientific problems. But it is also more than that. Because they touch upon questions of human value and the nature of existence, answers to this question are also fundamental to our[1] very culture and society: to our understanding of our own subjectivity and that of others, and to our concept of objectivity and the nature of reality around us (see Sperry, 1980, p. 205). Put bluntly, answers to these questions concerning mind and brain can close off connections to these broader issues, or they can open to them (Lestienne, 2022). It is these 'high stakes', epistemologically and ontologically speaking, that explain why Brown has been at pains throughout his career to develop an underlying framework broad enough to incorporate ever more observations and problems. It is this open and inclusive ambition that has enabled him gradually to expand the scope of his neuropsychological theory beyond aphasia caused by brain injury. One can observe this expansion of interest quite clearly in the series formed by Brown's many publications. We move – to consider just the first six books – from *Aphasia, Apraxia and Agnosia* (1972) to *Mind, Brain and Consciousness* (1977) to *Life of the Mind* (1988) to *Self and Process* (1991) to *Time, Will and Mental Process* (1996), to *Mind and Nature: Essays on Time and Subjectivity* (2000). To summarise all too crudely, first Brown's focus was expanded beyond aphasia to other disorders which he could show to be related (like the disordered action-development typifying the apraxias, and the disordered perceptions typifying the agnosias). Then, it was expanded beyond these to account for normal subjective experience (from awake consciousness to dream), including the nature of thought and belief, feeling and action, drive and value, truth and love. A final expansion culminates in consideration of time experience, creativity and aesthetic experience and the nature of the present as such. This gradual expansion ensures that Brown's theory, following a cue from the great William James, has the vision to systematise a wealth of assembled data and thus to avoid the premature systematisation of a meagre assemblage of problems (see Seghal, 2016; Stenner, 2011).

The World Itself as the Field of Battle: The Stakes of an Adequate Theory of the Mind/Brain State

My third introductory point is that Brown's trajectory of expansion is not the mark of an undisciplined and wandering mind, but a veritable battlefield upon which the nature and relevance of mind/brain is fought over. We should attend carefully, then, when Brown writes that 'in my view, the resolution lies in an adequate theory of what constitutes a mind/brain state' (Page 56). But we must not mistake this battle for the sabre-rattling of mere polemic. On this, Brown agrees with Bergson that 'time given to disputation is time lost' (Page 109). Those many 'ministers without portfolios' (Page 103) who expend their energy on mere critique-without-solution leave nothing in reserve for the real battle, which requires the slow and patient articulation of an alternative model of sufficient scope. For Brown, an adequate theory is one capable of recognising that 'the world itself should be the field of battle' (Page 56). This gnomic statement speaks volumes because it tells us not just about those *against* whom Brown thinks, researches and writes but also *why*. Here again, one must distinguish polemical disputation from the real battle of confronting entrenched views by means of a viable alternative model:

> I would not say the work developed out of opposition to cognitive science, or to localization approaches in neuropsychology. It rather took on shape naturally on its own, though many of the conceptual problems required confronting strongly entrenched views in both of these overlapping fields. Still, there was a rather hostile environment, and I well recall the many arguments, even the ridicule, at many scientific meetings. I didn't even find a receptive environment in the school of my former teachers…
>
> (Page 109)

If Jason Brown wants the *world itself* to be the field of battle for the understanding of the mind/brain state, then this is because of a tendency typical of these dominant paradigms to reduce the mental state to, at best, 'the isolation of decontextualised contents' (Page 56). The mental state, approached from a thoroughly *externalist* perspective, is treated as a mere internality. In this way, it is detached from and *isolated from the world.* Brown is scathing of the main 'tepid response to this preposterous claim' (Page 56), which is merely to point to the inability of externalist perspectives (which focus on observable physiology or behaviour) to describe this 'inner feeling'. In recurrently invoking 'qualia' and repeating the question 'what's it like' to be a mind, these tepid critiques merely re-affirm the problematic assumption that a mental state is a strictly interior content impenetrable to all but the one experiencing the qualia in question. For Brown, mental process is not to be reduced to the isolated experience of qualia. To repeat: the 'world itself should be the field of battle'. This concern, however, is not merely a matter of avoiding the extreme case of 'an elimination of mental properties altogether in the expectation that future neuroscience will fill the gaps' (Page 56). This sort of eliminative materialism, granted, is remarkably common today (alongside variants like 'illusionism'). But eliminating mental properties from consideration is not the main problem. It is merely an easy step to take following an earlier step of reducing the mental state to an isolated subjective experience of qualia. This earlier step too follows the prior step of an all too common strategy: 'to transpose the constituents of the world inward to the mind/brain such that the texture of an externalism prevails within the mind itself' (Chapter 2.2. The Mind/Brain State). Despite appearances, it is no contradiction to say both that mentality is reduced to qualia and that mentality is construed with the texture of an externalism. It is only by construing mind as if it were a little box (with the texture of an externalism) that one can imagine mentality on the model of qualia isolated in the box. From there, the third 'eliminative' step is all too easy because one can feel confident about ignoring the relevance of mere qualia. Qualia seem as far from 'the world itself' as it is possible to be.

The Front-Line Battle Is Against the Alliance of Localisation Approaches in Neuropsychology and Cognitivism

In their efforts to articulate a theory of 'what constitutes a mind/brain state', we see the steps noted above consolidate in the highly influential research paradigms associated with two of Brown's personal contacts: the cognitivism of George Miller and the connectionism of Norman Geschwind. It was the combination of these two paradigms that formed the approach that came to dominate psychology, cognitive science, neuroscience and philosophy of mind from the second half of the 20th century to the present. Miller was one of the originators of cognitivism in the USA (his 1956 paper on the information capacity of short-term memory quickly became a classic), and in 1978–79, he invited Brown to be Visiting Associate Professor at Rockefeller University to participate – along with others like Philip Johnson-Laird – in developing the field of cognitive psychology. Cognitivism involved a modelling of mental functioning with a 'texture of externalism', to use Brown's terms, borrowed from computing technology. Computer technology was one of the new and potent 'constituents of the world' available for inward transposition. The brain could then be conceived, not merely as a black box, but as a fixed structure corresponding to the hardware of a computer, and the mind, in turn, could be modelled as a flow diagram of the software assumed to overlay and drive the brain machinery, perhaps being discharged through it. This allowed for a new consideration of 'the mental' that had been discarded by behaviourism, but at the cost of a pallid conception of mind as software for processing binary symbols by means of fixed computational networks connected to functional processor modules on a circuit board. The 'experiences' construable as the 'content' of that software are necessarily of rather peripheral importance (and hence easily 'eliminable', as per 'step 3' above).

In turn, this cognitivist way of thinking of the brain as essentially a static circuit board fitted well with Geschwind's localisation approach to neuropsychology and his disconnection theory of aphasia. The history of aphasia, as Brown notes (Chapter 3.3. Action-Feeling and Self-Conscious Mind), is synonymous with the history of progressive brain localisation. Localisation theory has, however, remained contentious since Franz Joseph Gall made phrenology famous. Around 1800, Gall claimed he could differentiate amongst the chaotic folds of the cortex a number of specific mental functions like memory, speech and perception that – he speculated – were highly localised in 'cerebral organs' corresponding to physical lobes and structures of various kinds. Brown describes Pierre Paul Broca – who in the 1860s gave his name to 'Broca's area' (which is usually to be found in the frontal lobe of the left hemisphere) – as the first of the aphasiologists and the last of the phrenologists. Patients with damage to Broca's area seemed to be able to understand language but to struggle with speaking. Roughly a decade later, Carl Wernicke found a different but related deficit associated with lesions located somewhat at the threshold between parietal, temporal and occipital lobes. Patients with these lesions were able to speak but in a manner which suggested that they could not actually comprehend language. In 1968, Brown was sponsored by Geschwind for a post-doctoral fellowship in his famous Aphasia Unit at the Veteran's hospital in Boston. There he was exposed to Geschwind's approach, which was actually a revival of Wernicke's connectionist theory. Broca's area and Wernicke's area, for example, were taken to be the location of discrete modules specialised for the processing of different language functions. After Wernicke's area had dealt with language comprehension, the relevant information product could be sent to Broca's area for purposes of language production, and so forth.

The compatibility between Geschwind's connectionist neuropsychology and Miller's cognitivism is clear, because the localisations of connectionism lent themselves neatly to the growing interest in cognitive modularity (which, after massive funding in the USA, would reach a kind of zenith in the work of Jerry Fodor and Philip Johnson-Laird), whilst lending the scientific kudos of a grounding in brain biology. The new cognitivism encouraged an interpretation of conditions and symptoms as defects in the processing of sensory information somewhere *en route* (within the circuit board brain composed of connected processors of various kinds) from the machinic input of sense perception to output in the form of behaviour, thought or some other supposedly higher-level product. The brain's cognitorium starts with the pure data of sensation only to build up upon this the ever more complex cognitive constructions of conscious imagery, memory, language, thought and so on (as relevant data is detected for processing by specialised brain receptors, before being deposited in bins and boxes and conveyed to the next stage of assembly, etc.). For each of these specialist 'additions', a localisable processing module is posited (imagery might be created by one mechanism, thought by another). Perception itself tends to be considered a passive and unmediated matter of reception of (non-conceptual) sense data, whilst mental phenomena proper are secondary constructions which are progressively built up, using streams of available data as medium, through the interactive agency of various processing modules or faculties. For example, symptoms like auditory agnosias (disordered perceptions) might result from defects of auditory processing of information which arrives (via the ears) at primary brain regions before passing to secondary and tertiary regions. In these assumed 'higher' regions of association or integration cortex (associated with frontal and parietal regions), processing might occur by assembling multiple flows of sense data into more complex constructions.

This rapid history indicates that language has been the most localisable brain function. As Brown puts it, 'the thinking was that if one could not localise language, forget about localising anything else' (Page 103). With respect to language, before an utterance is possible, its meaning might be assembled by a module in the back of the brain before being sent to the frontal lobes where a different module might arrange for the movements necessary for its utterance.

Revisiting the Limits of the Dominant Model of the Mind/Brain as a Machine Composed of Encapsulated Modules for Processing Information Lodged on a Circuit Board

Brown describes the dominant approach sketched above as a rising 'tide' and laments that with the 'semblance of science offered by neuro-imaging techniques' it has become yet more pervasive and unquestionable over the last 3 decades or so. As noted, Brown's primary concern has been to build a model of the mind/brain state that might serve as a viable alternative to this dominant tradition. In fact, as we shall see in subsequent sections, Brown's microgenetic theory effectively reverses the answers given by this standard paradigm on a whole range of questions from the nature of perception, memory and emotion through the meaning of symptoms following brain damage to the account of the evolution and relevance of brain structure and function to mentality. But before introducing his alternative, I need to sketch why, for Brown and others, the standard view needed challenging, especially given its evident success in acquiring the status of amply funded and high prestige dominant paradigm. Essentially, it gets things, from Brown's perspective, the wrong way around because it has a number of significant limitations. We have already seen how it separates knowledge about the mind/brain from the 'world itself', basing its understanding upon an externalist mode of thought which ultimately reduces mind to a mere interiority easily discarded as epiphenomenal. But it has also blinkered observation of biological and psychological facts and constrained thought within narrow horizons in several other ways too. Here I note just five of its clear limits.

First, Brown gives the example of the widespread assumption that so-called association and integration cortex in frontal and parietal regions counted as the 'higher' brain regions (mediating the most complex aspects of human psychology) and that these, accordingly, must be the most recently evolved and expanded areas. This way of thinking allowed a good fit with the assumption of a linear 'circuit board' progression from more simple primary areas (responsible for the reception of immediate sense data) to secondary and tertiary areas (responsible for the assembly of complex additions to this basic data). Actually, as Brown (Page 104) points out, 'work by Bishop and Sanides showed that primary cortices were actually *more recent* in evolution than association or integration cortices'. This discovery *should* have challenged the assumed hierarchy of complexity whereby reception of sense data is considered the primary and simple starting point of a process of cognitive elaboration which moves from input, through the black behaviourist box now intricately chalked over with neuro-cognitive boxes and arrows, to output. Instead, the dominant computer model functioned to immunise against such rethinking. Second, and relatedly, the model encouraged a denial of the importance of biological reality because the 'software' associated with cognitive process was envisaged to run without intrinsic links to sub-servient brain structure. Questions of the materiality of the brain and the sequence of the evolutionary development of its structures could happily be considered more or less irrelevant to the running of its software.

Third and fourth, growing assumptions about the functionally encapsulated nature of assumed brain/cognitive modules produced two additional and related problems. On the one hand, structural relationships between different types of symptoms (e.g. the relations between symptoms of aphasia, apraxia and agnosia observed by Brown in his book from 1972) could be ignored or passed off as mere collateral damage effects that follow from the spatial proximity of radically different brain processors/modules. This meant the loss of relevant psychological data about the actual nature of symptoms (a problem worsened by the increasing preference for 'objective' measures and consequent downgrading of doctors' experience of patient reports). A frequently cited example is the presumed localisation of face recognition to mesial T cortex. Not only is there real interindividual variability in such anatomical location (Gao et al., 2022) but also a tendency to ignore symptoms other than prosopagnosia found by careful study to be associated with damage to this region, such as farmers unable to recognise their cows or pilots unable to differentiate airplanes (the latter was described to me by Jason Brown, *personal communication*). On the other hand, psychologists could happily proceed by articulating different models for each (supposedly discrete) function or phenomenon whilst ignoring (or derogating as metaphysical) the ambition of a broad underlying theoretical framework. In this way, advocates of the dominant model militated against the possibility of producing a theoretical framework broad enough to better explain the phenomena at hand.[2]

Fifth, and underlying the above points, the circuit board model is essentially static, as are the binary symbols processed as data by the system. By 'static' here I do not imply that this model is incapable of grasping that the data *move* as they are processed, or that the circuits might change mode. The point, rather, is the problematic assumption that real things (from the to-be perceived external objects, through the mechanisms of brain hardware and the software for cognitive processing, to the data themselves) are essentially substances, or states, or bits of matter, ultimately conceived as isolated externalities. To use Brown's preferred term, the dynamism here is of a purely 'externalist' kind (as with the so-called billiard ball model of Newtonian 'dynamics'). There is, in short, no *becoming* in this model, only the movement of internally static components within assemblages of such components. And, following from this, there is no serious account of the actual *togetherness* of the whole, beyond the mere assembly of parts. The *actual* brain, by contrast to this static, atomistic and externalist account, is a living, organic system, arising from a concrete history of situated emergence, and existing and developing as a dynamic flux of a continuous becoming in which each part is in a relation of mutual presupposition with the whole. This organic flux includes not just the rest of the body in which a given brain is embedded, but, the rest of the universe in which each body is embedded. This universe is a creative and relational *process*, in which novel forms arise – not thanks to some transcendent mechanic creator – but thanks to an immanent creative evolutionary process which can operate only with the existing actualities available, but which nevertheless produces novelty (the first fish, the first amphibians, the first reptiles, the first mammals, the first *homo sapiens*, etc.). And this expanding universe includes the products of human creativity that now cover the earth and impact its 'natural' processes to a degree that now warrants inclusion as a geological feature (the Anthropocene). In this respect, cognitive connectionism can be viewed as a re-entrenchment of modernist Cartesian/Kantian thinking, just at the point when this should have been, and largely was, overthrown and superseded by new 'postmodern' modes of process thinking.

Process Philosophy as Postmodern: A Detour to Better Situate Brown's Contribution

A little detour is needed to better situate Brown's research contribution in its proper philosophical and historical context. I have just invoked 'postmodernism' in full knowledge of the fact that most today consider this concept either *passé* or downright irresponsible (see the at times vitriolic descriptions in Griffin, 2007). In the sense that it is usually understood – i.e. taken from Lyotard's classic *The Postmodern Condition* (1979) – perhaps it *is passé* and irresponsible. But that sense was already understood at the time of its publication – especially by Lyotard himself – to be a partial oversimplification. Lyotard's 'report on knowledge' gives the impression that postmodernism is a cultural phenomenon of the third quarter of the 20th century which unfolds against an economic and political backdrop of economically globalising 'post-industrial' societies in which consumption gains priority over production as industry is outsourced to cheaper territory, and so forth. Just as 'modernity' (the socio-politico-economic epoch) is distinguished from 'modernism' (its cultural expression), so 'postmodernism' is the cultural expression of a 'postmodern' epoch. From Lyotard's rather Eurocentric 'French' perspective (albeit in a report initially addressed to Quebec), postmodernism 'happened' after the Second World War growth of post-industrial 'knowledge' industries. It was mainly characterised by the transformative impact of 'computing, cybernetics and theories of communication' on the conception and status of knowledge (Lyotard, 1979, p. 3). Although the primary focus of Lyotard's report concerned transformations within the natural sciences, it mainly influenced scholars in the humanities and social sciences. They took from it some variation on the message that 'grand narratives' are no longer plausible and are to be replaced, thanks to a semiotic turn to language, by a fragmentary multiplicity of groundless (Wittgensteinian) language games. Lyotard's initial focus on how computing, cybernetics and semiotics were transforming natural science was thus shifted to something more like a wholesale critique of natural science from a humanities and social science perspective. For these social scientists and humanities scholars who came to think of themselves as postmodernists, the truth claims of science were to be 'de-constructed' because they were part of the modern 'grand narrative' of humanity's self-liberation and progressive realisation of spirit through scientific progress. Excepting Lyotard's initial and subsequently neglected observations about the transformative relevance of computing, cybernetics and theories of communication, the appeal of this French notion of postmodernism to medically trained scientists like Brown was minimal at best, for obvious reasons, and notwithstanding his interest in poetry and the other arts.

The problem with this account and periodisation is that the notion of postmodernity borrowed by Lyotard had – as he clearly notes in the opening paragraph – already been in circulation for several decades, and not just within discussion of architecture and the arts. In fact, the original use of the term to characterise a historical epoch is traceable to the British Historian Arnold Toynbee (see Stenner and Nichterlein, *in press*). This use first occurred in Volumes 8 & 9 (1954) of his *magnum opus* 'A Study of History', the first Volume of which was published in 1920 and the last in 1961. Toynbee began developing these ideas around 1914. His focus in Volume 8 was not on modernism and postmodernism, but modernity and the 'postmodern age'. The modern age, to summarise Toynbee's vast historical scholarship, was essentially the combination, in the form of the supposedly sovereign nation state, of capitalistic economy and nationalistic politics. After several centuries of development, and most notably in Europe (where the dominant European nation states were in fact dependent upon massive colonial exploitation), this combination began to pull apart around 1875 and reached crisis point and collapse with the First World War and its aftermath (see Stenner and Andreouli, 2023). Taking this account seriously means that we must also revise our periodisation of postmodern*ism* if it is to be the cultural expression of a postmodern age.

A clue for this is provided if we take the leading forms of philosophical discourse as a proxy for cultural modern*ism* and postmodern*ism*. From that vantage point, we can follow and further Griffin's (2007) controversial suggestion that A.N. Whitehead (who Toynbee respectfully cites on a number of occasions) be considered a postmodernist philosopher.

Griffin's argument, however, lapses into the contradiction of defining that philosophy as a 'postmodern modernism'. This is largely because Griffin does not sufficiently develop the (post)modern*ity/ism* distinction and seems to overlook Toynbee's account of the periodisation of the actual historical societal shift from modernity to the postmodern age, which has obvious implications for the periodisation of postmodern*ism*. Characterising modernist philosophy for this purpose is complex but at least well-rehearsed. To simplify greatly, modern philosophy is the combination of the rationalism of Descartes with the empiricism of Locke (though Hume is no less important), particularly as synthesised in the 'settlement' effected in the epistemology of Kant, which continued its dominance – albeit with 'neo-Kantian' supplements – across most modern nations until roughly the last quarter of the 19th century. In his settlement, Kant famously took Newtonian physics as having provided access to the absolute reality of the natural laws that govern observable facts from behind the scenes (i.e. they are transcendent). It was this use of Newton as a standard that provided Kant with the basis for his famous critiques (Figure 0.1).

The *modernist* philosophy of Descartes, Locke and, especially, Kant thus had three characteristic features:

a It starts with *doubt* about any and all reality.
b It therefore puts the doubting/knowing *subject* at the forefront of any cultural, social or scientific consideration of the reality of *objects*.
c It addresses the problem of doubt by means of the method of a philosophical *critique* which proceeds by asking *critical* questions about the epistemic constructions of the subject before any claims to truth can be made about objects.

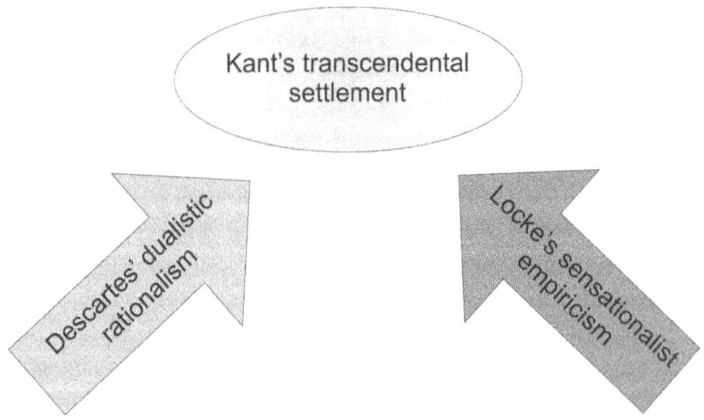

Figure 0.1 Kant's settlement of modern philosophy.

Newtonian (and Cartesian) physics provided the basis for *philosophical* critique because it provided an absolute and generalisable standard for truth claims. Newton also provided the model for Kant's famous distinction between experienceable but ultimately unreal *phenomena* and the absolutely real yet un-experienceable *noumena* that transcend mere appearance. So much is already implicit in Newton's insistence that what is real is not the stars and planets observable by the eyes, but the laws derived from the astronomical calculations their movements allowed: laws that, incidentally but fundamentally, for Newton, were clear evidence of a divine creator. Modernist philosophy was thus thoroughly defined by Newton's vision of a mechanistic 'clockwork' universe, the ultimate origins of which are beyond the concerns of classical physics (for which *points in space*, *particles of matter* and *instants of time* function as its triad of fundamental notions). The Newtonian system and its 'dynamics' are thoroughly static in the sense defined above: particles of matter (and their agglomerations) certainly move in measurable time across measurable space, but there is no account of becoming. Essentially, all creativity and becoming are delegated to the transcendent sphere, which is ultimately the 'top-down' sphere of a divine mechanic. In short, we can observe in the modern combination of Descartes, Locke and Kant the sources of each of the five limitations noted in the section "Revisiting the Limits of the Dominant Model of the Mind/Brain as a Machine Composed of Encapsulated Modules for Processing Information Lodged on a Circuit Board" .

If we now look to the half-century or so following 1875, we see two obvious developments in philosophical culture, both intimately related. Both are connected to the collapse in plausibility of this Newtonian standard at the heart of modernist philosophy which turned out not to be the final say on matters of physical truth. First, under the inspiration of the impetus given by Darwin to biology, we get the development of the so-called 'new psychology', which makes a problem of the rarefied notion of a sovereign thought-substance (residual in Kant's insistence that a scientific psychology is impossible because the transcendental ego cannot be mathematised). The most significant figure here was William James (though Dilthey is no less important). James' radical empiricism is the postmodernist equivalent to Locke's modernist empiricism. But James' empiricism, far from being static, takes as its premise the notion of flow, and in particular, his famous *stream of experience*. Second, we get the development of philosophies which reject and rethink the Newtonian assumptions about time, space and causality embedded in modern philosophy. Bergson's philosophy of creative evolution is the postmodernist equivalent to Descartes' modernist rationalism (though Nietzsche is no less important). But Bergson's intuitive rationalism takes issue with the spatial assumptions of Cartesian coordinates and launches a new notion of *duration* at the heart of a universe conceived to be a continuum in flux. Just as Kant integrated Descartes' rationalism with Locke's empiricism, so it was A.N. Whitehead who served to integrate James' bottom-up radical empiricism and Bergson's intuitive rationalism. In *Process and reality*, these were integrated into a fully fledged *organismic* (i.e. based on the new understanding of space as relational and irreducible to *points*) theory of *process* (based on the new understanding of temporality, irreducible to *instants*) for which particles of matter are replaced with *actual occasions* (also called *actual entities*) as the fundamental, irreducible (atomic) concept. From this perspective (i.e. the rethinking, just sketched, of the three fundamental modernist notions of *points in space*, *particles of matter* and *instants of time*), and consistent with Toynbee's periodisation of the postmodern age, what we can call for short '*process thinking*' is in fact the *principal expression of postmodernist philosophy* (Figure 0.2).

It is in this context that we can understand that the tide of cognitive neuroscience that began rising to dominance in the 1970s and 1980s, far from being postmodern, actually and in the main bolstered and re-entrenched modernist Cartesian/Kantian thinking. It was not accidental that this re-entrenchment was nourished in the nationalist/capitalistic framework of the new global super-power and with the opening to view of the vast unexploited territories of psychology and the brain, now increasingly thought to hold the keys to fundamental existential and societal questions. Furthermore, it developed just at the time that Lyotard was observing the transformative impact of 'computing, cybernetics and theories of communication' on scientific knowledge practices.

In short, insofar as he operated with modes of thought comparable to the process philosophies of James, Bergson and Whitehead, Brown's neuropsychology can thus best be characterised as *postmodern neuropsychology.* This little phrase 'operated with' need in no way imply that Brown *first* studied process philosophy and *then* 'applied it' in his research practice. Like all genuine process thinkers, it was necessary for Brown to arrive at his own formulations via his own empirical encounters with his own subject matter. Yet, inevitably,

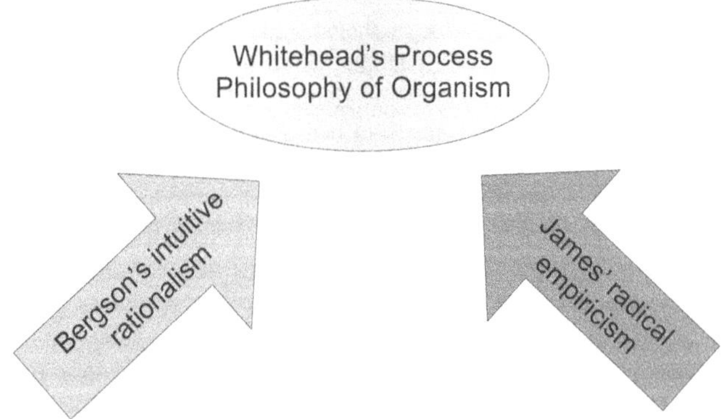

Figure 0.2 Whitehead's settlement for postmodern philosophy.

'along the way' he would come to recognise Bergson, James and Whitehead as inspirational intellectual soulmates. Indeed, since 2002, he and his wife Carine have hosted an annual meeting of process thinkers under the rubric of the Whitehead Psychology Nexus. I now address how Brown's microgenetic theory relates to James (Section "Continuities between Brown's Microgenetic Theory and James' Radical Empiricism ") and Whitehead (Section "Microgenetic Theory as Neuropsychology in the Key of Process: Continuities with Whitehead's Philosophy of Organism").

Continuities between Brown's Microgenetic Theory and James' Radical Empiricism

Brown uses the phrase 'mind/brain state' to capture the basic atomic entity (the fundamental building block) for consideration within neuropsychology, and so above all, we must examine this concept and situate it in the context sketched above. The word 'state' here is actually something of a misnomer (he often prefers the word *epoch*) because for Brown a given mind/brain state or epoch is never 'static' but always an *event:* something that *occurs* rather than a bit of matter that endures. Brown does not begin in modernist fashion either with matter (e.g. the neuronal substructure) or with some subjective feel (e.g. the notorious 'qualia') but with an event. What he calls *microgenesis* is the process of becoming of that event. The microgenetic process goes through various unconscious phases before reaching conscious completion (or falling short of so doing, perhaps being deviated by a lesion). After completion, it perishes, but only to make way for a newly arising mind/brain state which simultaneously renews its predecessor whilst also introducing novel discontinuities proper to its own present conscious moment in process of formation. We ordinarily take for granted our everyday conscious experience of a continuous world distinguishable from a continuous self. But when so analysed, this is revealed to be the complex, ongoing and ever-shifting macroscopic product of an underlying and ongoing microgenetic process involving the production of a series of mind/brain epochs, each internally complex. Although often seeming irrelevant at the macro level of everyday experience, the body and its brain are indispensable to each microgenetic event, although no microgenetic event is conceivable without some mental component. That mental ingredient might be the motivational vector of a drive impulse or its conscious formulation into a complex preference or desire based on memory.

Brown explicitly acknowledges his debt to William James and his notion of 'drops' or 'buds' or 'pulses' of experience. A brief detour via James (a founding father of psychology in the USA) is therefore helpful. In friendly dialogue with Bergson, James (1912, p. 22) was aware that modernist philosophy was 'on the eve' of a 'considerable rearrangement'. I dare to propose that no concept would become more important to that (postmodern) rearrangement than James' notion of 'drops of experience' (Stenner, 2011). Unlike Bergson, whose critique of modern philosophy insisted upon the fluid continuity of experience, James (from *Principles of Psychology*, 1890, onwards) articulated an account of what he called the 'stream of experience' that also *allowed for the divisibility of the continuity of that 'stream' into 'drops'*. He also used the term 'pulse' because with this analogy it is easier to grasp how the continuity of an animal's blood circulation is nevertheless divisible into pulses corresponding to heart beats. First, each atomic drop or pulse is an *indivisible unity*. Consider, for example, that it is not possible to have half a drop of water (or half a flower bud, to give a third favoured organismic analogy): they 'come totally or not at all'. Of course, once a bud exists, it can be chopped in half or into pieces, but that is a different matter than *its own organic growth process* (which the chopping *by a different organism* for its own purposes would obviously violate). Second, each internal process has 'certain units of amount bursting into being at a stroke' (James, 1911, p. 154). James is here articulating a radical new 'basic unit' of analysis which:

a is not a *static particle of matter* but an organic becoming;
b is not divisible or reducible to *points in space* but spreads extensively through connectivity; and
c is not divisible into *instants of time* but 'bursts into being'.

It is important to recognise that James begins the 'stream' chapter in *Principles* with a critique of the modernist empiricism of Locke and Hume. Locke's 'simple ideas' and Hume's 'perceptions', he suggests, have encouraged psychologists to assume that 'sensations' (sense data) are the building blocks of all experience (recall that sense data serve as the basic 'input' for the computer-based models described above). But James recognised that this is actually to abandon empiricism and empirical observation because, in fact 'no one has ever had a simple sensation by itself' (James, 1911, p. 154). James' new (postmodern) empiricism asserted that 'simple sensation' is no basic building block but in fact an abstraction *from* actual experience. If actual experience is more fundamental than sense data then, empirically, we cannot begin with 'simple sensation'. But we can all recognise as actual experience the fact of thinking itself (James used the word 'thinking' to refer to 'every form of consciousness indiscriminately). James, in sum, replaces the inert and externalist 'brick' of the sense datum with an organismic bud, pulse or drop. In this way, he reframes the philosophical problem of the relation between continuous 'one' and discontinuous 'many' by rethinking divisibility as a succession of (indivisible) pulses of experience, each of which arises from its predecessor while giving rise to its successor. The *relations* between 'buds' also take on importance, since – unlike the modern notion of indivisible atomic constituents – each bud arises from the relations it is able to develop and sustain with other entities.

Brown's microgenetic theory of mind/brain states carries exactly this insight forward whilst enriching it with empirical content derived from knowledge about brain evolution and development and the impact of damage on its functioning. Figure 0.3 (borrowed from Chapter 1.1) is a schematic depiction of a single 'pulse' constituting a mind/brain state yielding the perception of an object. The mind/brain state is Brown's basic unit of neuropsychological existence: the atom into which continuity can be viably divided. Mind and brain are here not separated but are different phases and ingredients of the same budding event. That is to say, physiologically speaking, the pulse arises in the brain stem and traverses limbic areas before reaching the most recent areas of cortex. Psychologically speaking, the pulse culminates in the experience of an external object having moved through prior phases of drive energy corresponding to core self (associated with long-term memory) and imagery associated with short-term memory. The psychological event of perceiving an object is thus the outcome of a series of endogenous phases that 'build to' that object, in the context of being shaped or 'sculpted' by the changing configuration of sensation deriving from the environment.

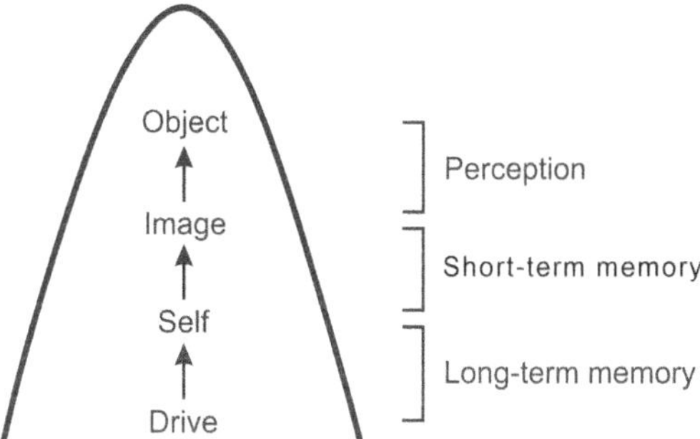

Figure 0.3 Schematic depiction of a hypothetical single mind/brain epoch.

As Brown makes clear, however, this model of a single mind/brain epoch is an abstraction. In actual fact, there can be no such event as a single pulse existing in splendid isolation (like the smile of Carroll's Siamese cat). The condition of existence for such a pulse is that it forms a transitive part of a continuing process of internal connectivity and connectivity with other entities. Figure 0.4 (borrowed from Chapter 2.2) depicts in schematic fashion how each pulse of experience organically arises from its predecessor while giving rise to its successor. The perception (D) at time Tn+3 is equivalent to the single 'pulse' depicted in Figure 0.3. The object perception (D) in the present of Tn +3 is the final phase of a mind/brain pulse whose culmination presupposes the prior phases of image (C),and core self (B & A).

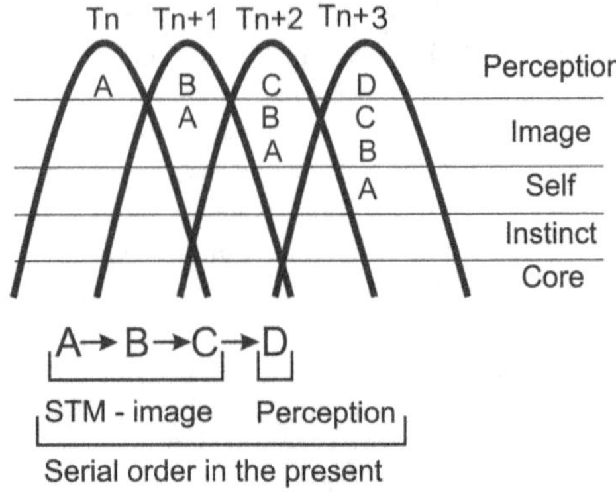

Figure 0.4 Schematic diagram of a wave of contiguous mind/brain epochs.

In this manner, the single pulse depicted at Tn +3 is composed out of phases corresponding to A, B, C & D (which themselves have roots in instinctual endogenous impulses modified by the connectivity with other entities that was carried forward by its predecessor). Tn +3 would not be possible were it not also constituted by its inheritance of the prior pulse at Tn +2 in its immediate past. Indeed, the decaying downwards slope of Tn +2 is embedded within the present of Tn +3. Tn +3 enacts an incomplete revival of Tn +2 whilst also being 'sculpted' in the course of its becoming by new sensations conveyed by the bodily senses. Hence, new perceptions arise as the present passes from A (at Tn) through B and C (at Tn +1 & +2) to D, as the present of the former pulse sinks deeper into the unconscious past with each new pulse (as illustrated by the diagonal formed by the four As). Only the tip of each wave crest is consciously experienced (and that as a *specious* continuity), the rest being unconscious experience.

James (1912, p. 26) called the flowing conjunctive relation described above, the *co-conscious transition*: the 'passing of one experience into another when they belong to the same self'. He considered it of utmost importance, stating that

> To be a radical empiricist means to hold fast to this conjunctive relation of all others, for this is the strategic point, the position through which, if a hole be made, all the corruptions of dialectics and all the metaphysical fictions pour into philosophy.
>
> (James, 1912, p. 26)

In my terms, James is here suggesting that the co-conscious transition is the key to the difference between modernist and postmodernist philosophy: all of the erroneous assumptions of modernistic philosophy were poured out through the hole made by the failure to recognise the co-conscious transition.

This insight that the stream of experience has the form of a co-conscious transition (as one bud of experience gives rise to the next) is also tightly related to James' rethinking of time and of the nature of self, both of which are advanced and fleshed out theoretically and empirically by Brown's microgenetic theory. The living 'I' of the self is the *present* which arises at the culmination of the pulse of each mind/brain state, but it has unconscious roots in the earlier phases from which this conscious phase emerged. In the 'perception of time' chapter of *Principles*, James invites his reader to reflect on their own experience of the present moment of time. He suggests that the reflection will yield the baffling conclusion that the 'present' forever melts away before we can encounter it. Hence, in fact, we can never experience a mere present appearing as an 'instant' existing, like a knife edge, between past and future. Following an expression used by his friend Clay, James calls such a deceptive present-as-instant a *specious present.* Contrary to this specious present, when addressing the experience of time, the datum of present experience always contains, as it were, both the past and the future, as when each of the notes in a piece of music, even those just past or just arriving, seem to be contained in the unity of a present chunk of 'duration'. James rejects the modernist notion of the present as the 'knife edge' of an *instant of time* as an 'ideal abstraction'. The present is always a *duration block* with a rearward and a forward-looking end: 'no knife edge, but a saddle-back, with a certain breadth of its own on which we sit perched, and from which we look in two directions into time' (James, 1890, p. 609). Only time conceived as a block of duration (a pulse of indivisible unity that bursts into being at a stroke) can serve to give rise to the organic continuity of the stream of consciousness, whilst retaining an organic unity of its own as a formative constituent within the flow.

The conscious 'I' that metaphorically sits 'perched' on the saddle of each temporal duration is neither Hume's bottom-up empiricist bundle of sensations lacking unity, nor Kant's transcendental ego supposed to synthesise the chaotic manifold of sense data 'top down' (from its Newtonian law-giving position beyond experience). Nor yet is it the divinely gifted 'soul' of Christian tradition debated so hotly during the Puritan foundation of Harvard and the early phase of modern psychology. Rather, James reaches the startling conclusion that the subject of thought arises, through a process of crystallisation giving birth to time, on the saddleback-present of each pulse of experience. *Thought*, he concludes, *is itself the thinker.* This experienced 'I' of experience does not consciously notice each pulse through which it is self-constituted for two reasons. First – as Brown makes explicit – because there is direct overlap between the waves of contiguous mind/brain states that form its saddle (yielding a sense of an 'underlying' continuity topped by an ever-changing perceptual display). Second because the pulsations of brain activity are too rapid to interfere with a unified and continuous experience of consciousness. Likewise, we do not notice the fast-moving flicker of frames when watching a film: 'In a movie, continuity requires a frequency of around 40 milliseconds per frame, which is close to the estimated duration of a mental state, thus the rate postulated for the replacement' (Brown, 2018, p. 89).

Microgenetic Theory as Neuropsychology in the Key of Process: Continuities with Whitehead's Philosophy of Organism

In this section, we must briefly grasp the debt Brown's theory of microgenetic 'epochs' owes to Whitehead, the Kant of postmodernity and the father of epochal time. To borrow a term from the neo-Platonic School, used by Deleuze to describe him in the context of his lectures on Leibniz, Whitehead was the *diadoche*, the chief successor (Deleuze, 1987). Like a pulse of experience succeeding its predecessor whilst creatively adapting it to new times, Whitehead transformed the philosophy he inherited from the moderns. I will therefore try to convey something of the scale and scope of Whitehead's philosophical project the better to propose that Brown's neuropsychology is 'postmodern' in so far as it takes forward the scientific implications of this radical change from substance to process. But the reader should not receive from this the message that James or Whitehead or Brown have resolved the problems they have addressed. It is better to say that they have come to an enhanced understanding of the nature of these problems by overcoming modes of thought that, whilst useful and successful in their day, proved an obstacle to that more encompassing vision. Indeed, Whitehead (1924, p. 2) expressed 'an immense distrust of all-inclusive neat systems which profess to finish up the philosophical problem in well-chosen explanations', and he admired that James protested throughout his entire career 'against the dismissal of experience in the interest of system' (Whitehead, 1938, p. 4).

After a long and successful career as a mathematician, logician and theoretical physicist, and after he had achieved the status during the 1920s of the most distinguished anglophone philosopher of science, Whitehead was invited to take up a Chair in Philosophy at Harvard at the age of 63 to complete his career as a fully fledged philosopher. In his first lecture, given in 1924, he swiftly and boldly defined the task of philosophy in quite 'psychosocial' terms as 'revealing and rationalising the inner preoccupations of humanity' (Whitehead, 1924, p. 2). Philosophy 'emphasises those relations of things which fill the mind of an age'. For this reason, the philosophy of any given age is stamped with characteristic preoccupations of its day, serving as a kind of 'autobiography of its Time-Spirit'. The Time-Spirit in Cambridge (both in Cambridgeshire and in Massachusetts) circa 1924 was a general preoccupation with the pre-suppositions of science. This is because the fundamental conceptions of science were, right then, 'in process of re-constitution'. To supply some context, this lecture took place two years after Whitehead had written his book *The Principle of Relativity* which reformulated Einstein's theory of gravitation to de-couple it from the proposed curvature of the notion of space-time that Einstein had taken-over from Minkowski (Whitehead having personally discussed this issue with Einstein the previous year), and it was one year before Heisenberg, Born and Jordan produced the first consistent formulation of wave or 'quantum' mechanics (a problem addressed that same year of 1925 in Whitehead's *Science and the Modern World*). Together, general relativity and quantum mechanics – despite building upon Maxwell's field-theoretical unification of electro-magnetism (with which equations Whitehead was intimately familiar) – shocked the long-cherished assumptions of modern physics, whilst leaving physics in a state of disunity. By 1927, for instance, Einstein considered Quantum theory an incomplete account of physical reality. Until science can be rationalised, wrote Whitehead in his opening lecture from 1924, 'we cannot lie easy in our philosophic beds'.

Whitehead began this lecture expressing his honour to be lecturing to an audience whose senior portion will have listened to William James. A great insight into Whitehead's philosophy is gained if it is recognised that: (a) he took enormous inspiration from James' account of consciousness, self and time as an unfolding series of pulses forming the stream of co-conscious transition; (b) that he deepened this paradoxical theory of subjective continuity by means of discontinuous 'pulses' by generalising it to all natural processes; and (c) this was undergirded by the development of an epochal theory of time that systematised the notions of time as duration developed by Bergson and James (see Stenner, 2011). The basis of these was Whitehead's deep knowledge of mathematical physics. For example, Whitehead (1925, p. 46) immediately saw in the new quantum mechanics a 'startling discontinuity of spatial existence' which, if borne out (which it has been) demands a revision to 'all our notions of the ultimate character of material existence'. Crudely, an electron behaves like a strange car which, although it travels on average at 30mph, nevertheless appears only successively at a series of milestones on the journey (remaining at each milestone for two minutes), whilst disappearing at each other point of the road in between. Rather than continuously traversing its path in space, an electron appears discontinuously,.i.e. only at a series of discrete positions, each of which it occupies for a particular duration of time. Whitehead could explain this strange behaviour of electrons by showing that these entities, and others like protons and neutrons, are in fact not static bits of matter, but organised systems of energy (actual occasions). Energy is *vibratory* and vibrations are waves with particular frequencies. Light, for example, consists of waves within the electromagnetic field, and the number of its crests that pass a specified point in one second (i.e. its frequency) determines – in conjunction with a suitable perceptual system – a definite colour of the spectrum. A given molecule, when excited, vibrates at a given set of frequencies, and these vibrations stir up waves of the same frequency within the surrounding field, as they carry away the energy at play (indeed, if sufficiently shocked, a sub-atomic particle will dissolve into light). Quantum theory shows that these vibrations cannot, as might be assumed, be stirred up to any intensity: minimum amounts of energy are required, and these cannot be subdivided. It is as if one could only buy energy by the Euro's worth. A Euro's worth of energy is the minimum amount accepted, and so any intensity less than that yields nothing because it has no 'purchase'. Suitably extrapolated, this would be the basis of an explanation for the discontinuous electron path. Because at the atomic and sub-atomic level we are not dealing with static substances but with energy vibrations (i.e. electrons, protons, etc., are organised systems of vibratory streaming of energy), so the condition of an electron's 'appearance' on its path (and its unexpected 'lingerings' at successive 'milestones') would be that it pass through a complete period of its cycle. Take the radiation of light from a particle that, in an experimental set-up, has been excited by a collision. Roughly speaking, following a complete light-wave cycle, the system is restored to its formal state and primed to emit the next wave to follow. Whitehead could thus see, at the most elementary level of physics, a direct analogue to what James had seen at the level of the co-conscious transition. Namely, once one has abandoned the unsustainable notion of a real 'instant' of time and a real 'point' in space, then one has instead the concept of a duration block composing an 'indivisible unity' characterised by 'certain units of amount bursting into being at a stroke' (James, 1911, p. 154). Whitehead called this an 'epoch' and made it the basis of his new epochal theory of time. In sum, at the level of the ultimate entities of physics, Whitehead finds something analogous to James' living pulses or buds of experience and finds an analogous solution to the problem of how continuity can co-exist and be formed out of discontinuity. This solution, remarkably, applies not just to the rarefied atmosphere of human consciousness but is generalisable to nature 'all the way down'.

For Whitehead, this development in science opened the entire field of philosophy to a new processual and organismic mode of thought which must 'take the place of the materialism with which, since the seventeenth century, science had saddled philosophy' (Whitehead, 1925, p. 47). And it is not accidental that physics and psychology would prove significant battle-grounds for the new 'postmodern' rationalisation of science (explaining why the birth of psychology took place in exactly the historical phase Toynbee identified as the waning and break-down of the modern era). In short, what applies at the level of conscious experience and at the quantum level of sub-atomic physics applies throughout nature (see Stenner, 2022). This was the historical point at which Whitehead – armed with his epochal theory of time and confident that even the *endurance* of atoms was a function of reiterative *occurrences* – was ready to entirely re-cast materialist substance thought in terms of processes by developing his startlingly new *Philosophy of Organism.* At its core was a new fundamental concept (and concept of fundamentals) which – as fully acknowledged in Chapter 2 of *Process and Reality* – extended James' 'bud' or 'drop' notion of experience to the entirety of nature: the *actual occasion*.

> 'Actual entities' – also termed 'actual occasions' – are the final real things of which the world is made up. There is no going behind actual entities to find anything more real.
>
> (Whitehead, 1928, p. 18)

I hope to have shown the direct family resemblance between Brown's microgenetic mind/brain state, James' bud of experience and Whitehead's actual occasion. The notions of 'act', 'actuality' and 'actualisation' evoked by the expression '*actual* occasion' are, of course, quite deliberate, as are the distinctions 'actuality' implies between 'potentiality' and 'reality'. In this context, I briefly note the compatibility between Brown's distinctive neuropsychological notion of microgenesis and Werner's (e.g. 1937) use of the same term as an extension to the Leipzig Gestalt psychologists' concept of *Aktualgenese*. This was the method of evoking the birth and development of percepts in laboratory settings so that the process of actualisation of these novel phenomena could be traced (see Graumann, 1959). Werner's microgenetic technique extended this method to the genesis of developmental competences, and this in turn inspired some of Vygotsky's work on zones of proximal development (1978). This microgenetic approach continues in the work of contemporary developmental psychologists (see Lavelli et al., 2005) and cultural psychologists who apply it to microscopic scenes of communication (e.g. Salvatore, 2012). Brown's use of it to describe the genesis and development of mind/brain epochs is thus one distinctive and important application of a notion that applies to *all* varieties of actual occasion (from the physical through the chemical and biological to the psychocultural). The broad idea of *Aktualgenese* is that things become 'actual' through a process involving the 'realisation' of 'potentiality'. Incidentally, in his book *Physics and Philosophy,* Werner Heisenberg (1958, p. 180) observes that the 'language actually used by physicists when they speak about atomic events produces in their minds… the concept of "potentia"'. The philosophical roots of the notion of microgenesis, however, go back further than Werner and Heisenberg to Whitehead. In *Process and Reality*, Whitehead distinguishes between two types of flux or process, one 'microscopic' and the other 'macroscopic' and he calls the first the *concrescence* and the second the *transition*. In Figure 0.5, I have superimposed Whitehead's distinction onto one of Brown's diagrams to illustrate its compatibility (Brown usually operates with this distinction only implicitly, and so making it explicit might prove useful to those wishing to explore these connections between the two vocabularies):

Whitehead calls the first (microscopic) type of flux the *concrescence*. Concrescence is the *becoming concrete* of an actuality (as prior potentials are differentially selected, some rejected, some accepted for realisation).

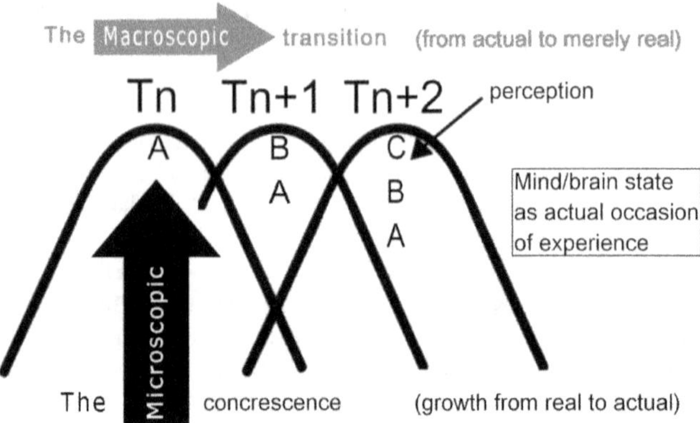

Figure 0.5 Schematic diagram illustrating Whitehead's micro/macro distinction in relation to Brown's. microgenesis.

The concrescence, in Brown's terms, would be the process through which a given mind/brain state comes into existence via its various phases (here C, B and A), culminating in the perception of an external(ized) object (mind/brain states, being both 'sensory' and 'motoric', can also culminate in acts, including specialised acts like utterances). Whitehead also identifies three broad phases in the concrescence of a complex actual occasion: the responsive phase (in which an objective datum from the actual world is received or physically 'felt' as the basis for the new occasion), the supplemental stage (in which the datum is felt 'emotionally') and the satisfaction (in which the process comes to completion and perishes, taking the form of one more complete actuality within the actual world). This supplemental stage occurs through a process Brown describes as the 'parsing' or 'sculpting' away of a mass of potentials, leaving only those potentials fit for actualisation. This microscopic process is, as it were, 'internal' to a given mind/brain epoch. It is the mind/brain epoch 'viewed' from the 'subjective' perspective of its own becoming. It is the internal constitution of a particular actual entity. The outcome of the process of concrescence is the mind/brain epoch itself (which in this sense is better called a *super*ject than a *sub*ject), along with its perception of the world beyond it. The 'world beyond' it, however, is actually composed of all those other actual entities that find themselves *objectified* through and in the concrescence. What enters the concrescence is not 'external' objects as they exist in their own formal reality, so to speak, but objects as they are *for* the concrescing mind/brain epoch, or as *objectified* by its processes of feeling (or prehension). As actualities in themselves, these objects have or had their own 'formal existence'. But as potentialities for prehension into the concrescence of another actual occasion, they have only 'objective existence'. The microgenetic process of concresence thus repeats in microcosm what the wider world is in macrocosm.

That macrocosmic wider world is however the already actualised world of the past. As such, it exists as a potentiality for a new concrescence, and through the concrescence, the merely real becomes an actual present. The present is thus the immediacy of this microscopic process – experienced by the occasion going through it (and towards its 'satisfaction') – whereby *reality* becomes *actual*. In sum, the microscopic concrescence is a growth which departs from the 'real' and arrives at the 'actual'. This is Brownian microgenesis.

The second type of fluidity or process, indicated on the figure by the smaller horizontal arrow, Whitehead names *transition*. The concrescence and the transition presuppose each other and both are necessary for a full account of process, not as a stage play about reality, but as the becoming of the actual world. Where concrescence grows from real to actual, transition moves from actual to merely real or, to put the same thing differently, from *attained* actuality to actuality *in attainment*. The realised actuality which is the product of concrescence is an entity that has perished with its satisfaction: all of its potential energy at play in the concrescence has been used up and converted into concrete actuality. But a concrete actuality is merely a potential for the next concrescence and so, like a baton in a relay race, it is picked up and passed on, this passage being *transition*.

The process of *Process and Reality* is, in short, the combination of concrescence and transition. The living present of actualisation is thus forever perishing, but in so doing, it lays down one more actuality for an actual world which provides the conditions which really govern the attainment of the next concrescence. The macrocosm – which Whitehead associates with the word *organism* – is the actual universe at a given stage of its expansion. The microcosm is the process whereby the universe – conceived as an 'incompletion in process' – expands (because something new is added in each concrescence). And here, we find Whitehead's distinctive meanings of past, present and future. The past is a deposit of actualities. The future is reality without actuality (it is virtual). The present arises in the process of future reality becoming actual (and hence taking its place in the past).

The Future of an Archaeology of Present Experience

> Thought is kind of an archaeology of perception since objects are externalized concepts, their objectifications as it were, while object-concepts are themselves realizations of yet deeper categories.
>
> (Page 111)

I noted in the opening paragraph what I called a paradoxical counter-gravitational movement from downstream to upstream within Brown's thought and work. I suggested that this amounts to an *archaeology of experience* which effectively reverses a number of assumptions core to the dominant paradigm described in the section "The Front-Line Battle Is Against the Alliance of Localisation Approaches in Neuropsychology and Cognitivism". Before concluding, in this final section, I will flesh out this point with some illustrations which may help the reader to better appreciate some of the future impact Brown's neuropsychological application of microgenetic theory should have within psychology, neuroscience and philosophy. Hopefully, Sections "Process Philosophy as Postmodern: A Detour to Better Situate Brown's Contribution", "Continuities between Brown's Microgenetic Theory and James' Radical Empiricism" and "Microgenetic Theory as Neuropsychology in the Key of Process: Continuities with Whitehead's Philosophy of Organism" above have provided some of the philosophical background needed in order to understand how these 'reversals' are consistent with what I am calling Brown's 'postmodern' stance: his rejection of the substance thought that still implicitly shapes the leading paradigm, and his embracement of the process thinking of James and Whitehead (for reasons of space, I have not discussed at length Brown's equally relevant engagement with Bergson).

In the special case of neuropsychology, thinking processually has meant – as we have seen – that Brown rejects the current 'externalist' manner of modelling mind/brain on computing devices and construing structure and function in terms of a network of anatomically localised processors performing discrete tasks (albeit with all complications of parallel processing). In place of this, he develops a process model for which brain 'locations' are phases in a flow of activity which spreads via consecutive overlapping 'pulses' – each lasting a fraction of a second – from bottom-up. But bottom-up here relates both to the brain morphology laid down during ontogeny and to the evolutionary process through which the structure of brain anatomy was laid down during phylogeny. Hence, in a short pulse (short in terms of clock-time), the mind/brain epoch goes through a microgenetic process of becoming whose concrescence, as it were, retraces formations laid down in the evolutionary epoch and the epoch of individual development. In its passage 'up' through archaic to more recent structures, and 'out' across the spread of the brain, the mind/brain epoch successively individuates in a process of increasing refinement which leads, on satisfaction, to an object (or act).

At each of these radically different epochal time scales, the 'mechanism' for this refinement is the same. Note also that this process is not a question of building assemblages from bricks of substance but almost the reverse: a selective winnowing of possibilities to yield an integrated concrete actuality. The mechanism is essentially a synthesis of Darwinian/Whiteheadian principles. In crude summary, it involves combining: (a) a means for the generation of vast potentiality followed by (b) its winnowing into actuality via a process of selectivity against the constraints of an actual world composed of diverse organisms and (c) some means of recording the resulting adaptation for future iteration and continued refinement as the cycle continues.

Phylogenetic formation. Darwin explained speciation at a phylogenetic scale in terms of: (a) mutation mechanisms for multiplying potentiality of form and function, (b) the derivation of species by a process of 'selecting' better adapted individuals in a competitive environment and (c) the genetic preservation mechanism was discovered in the 20th century ('the same cat over and over, like transformations with some novelty over evolutionary time' (Chapter 4.1 Microgenesis and the Mind/Brain State (interview)).

Ontogenetic formation. The phylogenetic process takes millions of years, but the ontogenetic dimension of individual brain morphogenesis over months and years is explained by a refinement of the same process: (a) the fetal brain generates massive cell and connection production, the potentiality of which is (b) trimmed during post-fetal growth to yield a more localised set of functions adapted to the behavioural and cognitive demands of the infant's environment and (c) the resultant functional structurations serve as the formal basis for the mind/brain states they subsequently carry onwards and upwards.

Microgenetic formation. Finally, taking the microgenetic production of object perception (or act production) over a fraction of a second we begin: (a) with vast unspecified potentialities in the phase of volatile 'imagery' structured by shifting vectors of drive energy, (b) this potentiality for diverse object-formations is then progressively trimmed and sculpted in an environment of sensory constraints (provided by the environment of sense data deriving from the various organs of the body) such that *inhibition* of all but *this* 'external' object (or act) yields an outcome conforming to the actual world that perception seeks, while (c) the resultant 'object categories' serve as attractors for the future construction of comparable objects.

Because these variations of a *single process* underlie all three dimensions of becoming, Brown is able to 'join the dots' between them. Hence, the importance of *phylogenetic formation* is less that it gives us a brain with fixed structures and functions, and more that it gives us a flexible brain full of 'plastic' potentiality for further sculpting in the form of the *onto*genetic medium. This flexibility provides a new medium which allows the process of the creation and laying down of form to continue over a shorter time-scale, during the early life of each individual. The importance of this subsequent ontogenetic or *morphogenetic formation*, in turn, is not just that it gives us 'a brain that outputs function' (p.158), but that it too provides a new medium through which form can continue to be created and laid down over the even shorter time-scale of mentality and action. The trajectories of fetal growth are thus carried forward into maturity as the lines of formed experience and formed action, i.e. within the media proper to *microgenetic formation.*

Because Brown is able to grasp the full temporal flow of process relevant to the mind/brain state, so too is he able to understand and theorise the crucial possibilities at play in the *interruption* of these flows at various points. This insight underlies the novelty of his approach to two issues which I will only briefly highlight here in the hope that they will not escape the reader's attention. First, the meaning and relevance of symptoms of brain damage and second the role of neoteny in the creative advance.

For the first, I refer the reader to the excellent overview provided by Maria Pachalska and Bruce Duncan MacQueen (2005). Essentially, symptoms are not indicators of damage to a discrete processor. Rather the physical damage (to the neurological medium laid down in ontogenesis) *interrupts* the microgenetic process of the forming mind/brain state as it moves from archaic to new, depth to surface, drive to object. In so doing, it reveals the usually hidden phases in the distinct medium through which it passes and by which it is formed, much as an archaeologist reveals by excavation a particular stratum of earth containing tools, bones or other items during a dig. Those earlier phases are usually hidden because under normal circumstances they give way to, and are transformed by, later phases. This means that what is revealed as a symptom is not simply an anomaly proper to a deficit – neither an alien presence nor a gaping absence – but the exposing of 'raw' phenomena that are ordinarily transformed by the subsequent phases interrupted by the lesion. It reveals, as it were, the media sub-serving as preconditions for normal cognition and action. Because the brain has itself evolved through various phases during speciation (although a self-conscious simplification, MacLean's (1990) account of the Triune brain in evolution has convincingly distinguished three layers corresponding in the long durée to reptile, paleomammalian and mammalian phases), tissue damage at different layers, in disturbing distinguishable neurological media, will result in different symptom experience (for a summary, see Pachalska and MacQueen, 2005, pp. 99–101). Symptoms, adequately interpreted, reveal earlier phases of the underlying process of microgenesis, revealing its structure and the process of its structuration, or perhaps bringing the mind/brain epoch to actualisation in a premature satisfaction (Brown and Pachalska, 2003).

Second, the above-noted prematurity of a mind/brain epoch that can be engendered by lesion can also arise productively through the evolutionary mechanism of *neoteny* through which development is slowed or suspended at a premature or juvenile phase allowing for a leap in availability of potentiality. This is discussed in the current volume in Chapter 2.1. Consider that the amphibian brain of a frog functions such that the sight of a fly is simultaneous with the flying out of its tongue. The cycle from afferent percept to efferent behaviour occurs as a reflex with minimal mental mediation. The cycle quickly closes to completion, as it were. The so-called paleomammalian brain that emerged in evolutionary time affords the creatures possessed by it a further degree of elaboration between perception and behaviour. One might say that it affords the possibility of *holding the cycle open for longer*, creating space for the emergence and consideration of likes and dislikes mediated by a limbic system. Later still in evolutionary time, the intricate and seamless outer folds that form the medium of the mammalian cortex afford a further delay or suspension at the microgenetic level, enlarging the temporal thickness of the possible 'now' and creating the possibility for outrageous novelty in comparison to simple reflex.

Each of these leaps of evolutionary development and sophistication, it appears, is the effect of a *slowing or retarding of the process through which the mind/brain epoch comes to completion.* This is directly analogous to the observation of a prolongation (well into the post-natal period) in human beings of the fetal stage of rapid brain growth. This is accompanied by another neotenous 'opening': the closure of the human cranial sutures is postponed till after birth to allow the later brain growth and also to make the large-headed baby's passage through the pelvic canal more feasible. Both of these amount, at a microgenetic level, to a recapturing of brain potentialities otherwise lost. The enhanced brain plasticity that results in turn allows for what Proust called the recapture of lost time. Each 'neotenous leap' corresponds to a liminal phase in which a formable medium of one type is modified in a manner sufficient to sustain new forms, rendered improbable in the prior medium, but not impossible (see Stenner, 2017).

Conclusions

I will conclude this introduction with a few examples of 'Brownian reversals' of long-cherished assumptions about perception and memory, emotion and value, thought and language and truth and imagination.

First, Brown emphasises that the perceived externality of an object is the terminal product of the process of a mind/brain state. The objectivity of objects, from this perspective, is not a given with which the process of experience might start, rather the 'externality of the object' is the temporary product of an accomplishment. For Brown, our experience of external objects is first of all a shifting set of forms in the medium of brain activity.

Second, this means that the experienced object *incorporates* a process in its very constitution. If the object arose from a selective parsing of a buzzing field of imagery and by means of basic forms of categorisation lured by feelings, then 'imagery' and 'thought' are not *added* to an object but are part of it. They are phases that form its preconditions and, although stripped away in its 'sculpting' and transformed by later phases, they remain a part of it, either vestigial or still prominent. For the archaeologist of experience, the object has its own proper infrastructure of implicit concepts, images and feelings, and these can be carefully explored.

Third, this opens up a perspective on memory which reverses the usual assumption that memory follows perception and takes the externalist form of the 'recording' – in a specialised module – of the 'trace' of a once immediate percept (whilst forgetting is construed as trace decay or damage). Grasped microgenetically, memory necessarily *precedes* object perception as one of its preconditions. It is the function of memory to *become perceptual*. But, contrarywise, perception, as it ebbs and perishes, or as it is interrupted, can sink back to memory and fades into memory. Furthermore, the principle of neoteny (whereby early phases in the concrescence are revived and accentuated) would suggest that a liminal leap (securing lost potentiality) would accrue to an organism capable of slowing or *suspending* the transition from memory to perception, and lingering in memory and on memories. Something similar applies to imagination.

Fourth, the familiar model assumes the adventure of a percept as it voyages from sensory immediacy into short-term memory and then into long-term memory where it might linger as an accessible trace or else decay. But if each object is the product of its own prior process of objectification, then the micro-history of its passage moves *first* through long-term memory *before* traversing short-term and iconic memory. For the archaeologist, the object thus incorporates within its infrastructure the diachronic history of its passage. It is only once these stages have yielded the object of a superject that they can then be recovered (or revealed as symptoms): in 'the reverse order of their traversal'. Forgetting is poorly grasped as trace decay. It is an incomplete revival: an incapacity to swim upstream from the object.

Fifth, dream (see Chapter 1.2) is not composed out of the memories of perceptions. Rather dream is the product of a mind/brain state that cannot reach perception because it cannot pass to the externality of an object. The passage is blocked because, having shut our eyes and retreated from wide-awake consciousness, the potentiality of earlier imagistic phases of the mind/brain state cannot be sculpted-to-objectivity by the harsh selective environment provided by available sense data. Again, and as with hallucination (sometimes provoked by lesions), early phases of the epochal pulse are accentuated, and again, there is a rich neotenous potential – as well as danger – in the capacity to 'return' to such states (as richly exploited by all arts and most mind-altering drugs). Again, this shift from dream to 'reality' is best grasped as a liminal passage ('the arousal of a self at the liminal boundary of the mental state is fundamental and essential to the occurrence of all other contents' (Chapter 2.1. Origins of Subjective Experience)).

Sixth, as discussed in Chapter 3.1, there is scope for reversing the usual assumption that emotions are adaptive or maladaptive internal responses to external circumstance. Most models of emotion begin with the 'event' of some form of sense data serving as a 'trigger' being inputted into a box, the output of which is an emotion. One reads the news, loses hope, is filled with despair and weeps on the phone to one's mother. Because of their evident complexity, emotions are construed as syndromes or complex response systems. Following input, the box is thus typically populated with connections between multiple processors construed as organised sub-systems or modules (ideally with some indication of their brain location) corresponding to the usual suspects like: a motivational sub-system (supplying the drive for 'action tendencies'); an autonomic sub-system (supplying physiological arousal); a monitor system (supplying the arousal to be 'felt'); a higher cerebral sub-system (supplying 'cognitive appraisal'); a motor system (supplying facial smiles and grimaces, bodily postures and actions) and so forth (see Stenner, 2015). Again, all of this must be reversed once it is recognised that the 'event' is not some unspecified external input but the becoming of one mind/brain state after another in the context of unfolding encounters in a world that is actual. We feel the world emotionally *before* we perceive it objectively, objective perception being itself a form of feeling that results from a parsing or fractionation of prior phases. Brown adds the insight that two distinguishable aspects of emotion (its intensity and its quality) derive from a combination of early phases in the becoming of an object (which involves the categorical refinement of qualities) and early phases in the becoming of an act (which involves the refinement of intensity by feelings): 'An emotion points to revived and accentuated (neotenous) segments embedded in the final actuality, taking on its qualitative attributes from submerged layers in the inciting perceptual experience, and its qualitative intensity from earlier levels in action' (Chapter 3.1. From Drive to Value).

Enough has been said to convey the profundity of Brown's theoretical approach and the 'Brownian reversals' it makes possible. I leave it to the reader to explore the more subtle nuances of Brown's reformulations of values, ethics and aesthetics, topics which neuroscientists are often very reluctant to broach, despite it being long recognised that these spheres too are impacted by brain damage. The consistent take-home message – applicable also to aesthetic taste and ethical judgement – is that these fall into the realm of 'mental process' and, as such, are first of all a matter of selection for actualisation amongst a population of potential contenders. Note that this mode of thinking also reverses the conventional 'assembly' model which involves, not trimming down, but building up representations of reality out of sensory building blocks. Contrary to this static building block model, each object, thought, memory, imagination or emotion that we experience, and each action or utterance became what it turned out to be thanks to a microgenetic process of becoming through which a veritable cloud of potentiality evaporated into just this drop of concrete actuality: microgenetic becoming, in each case, yields being.

In a manner that is strictly analogous, the actuality of this book was sculpted and culled by a selective process applied to an output of some 230 articles and 20 books written over Brown's long career. Denys Zhadiaiev was the final sculptor of the form of this work, which is arranged into six chapters divided into three main sections, the first on time, the second on subjectivity and the third on thought and value. I have written short introductions to each of these sections. Appended in a fourth section are three interviews with Brown conducted by David T. Bradford. These provide important background to Brown's *oeuvre*. As for this introduction, I agreed to write it because I consider Brown's work to be of enormous value to psychology, and because I consider psychology to be of enormous value to philosophy and to the cultural life of today's society. An area ripe for further development is the further introduction of the so far largely absent dimension of *sociogenesis*. This dimension – much like the earlier discussion of modernity – would place the stakes of these arguments in temporal epochs of world-historical scale, millennia being nested – as it were – between phylogeny and ontogeny, and lending cultural form to each microgenetic epoch.

Notes

1 Exactly who this 'our' refers to is an open question, not a crass assumption.
2 'The basic idea, which is the foundation block for microgenetic theory, is that the progression from semantics to phonology in language, from object concept to object form in perception, and from action plan to implementation in motor behavior, is not only identical in all three domains, but also identical in the relation to stages in the evolution of the forebrain'. (Pachalska, 2012).

Part 1

Time

Introduction to Section 1: Time

Paul Stenner

A re-thinking of time as passage or process is, as the name suggests, at the very heart of process thinking. The scientific materialism that is critiqued by process thinkers like Brown assumes an absolute theory of time. For materialists, matter occupies a specifiable point in space during a given instant of time, and space and time are the dimensions that allow clear measurements. But time treated as absolute is thereby excluded from the real passage of nature.

In the two chapters making up this first section, Brown offers an account of the mind/brain state as an iterated 'becoming-into-being' and hence as part and parcel of the broader passage of nature. Each mind/brain state is a process arising from its immediate past and passing into what will become its successor. This means that there is no such thing as a single mental state occurring only in the now of an instant. When we think about such a thing, we are entertaining an abstraction of thought. As an abstraction of thought, a single mind/brain state is therefore not the kind of thing that can generate and sustain a 'present'.

When at the start of Chapter 1.1 Brown writes of 'subjective time', he is therefore including the subjective experience of the present *within* a broader account of the passage of nature. The subjectivity proper to the percipient occasion (i.e. the actual occasion 'having' the subjective experience) is, from his perspective, *part of* the passage of nature and possible *only on its basis*. Time is not the absolute form that Kant, relying on Newton, took it to be: something necessarily beyond experience and transcending nature. Rather, it arises only within and on the basis of natural processes. In the following two chapters, Brown gives us insight into *how* this happens. The first, 'On the nature of the present' is based on an article first published in *Process Studies* (Brown, 2018), whilst the second 'Time and the dream' was originally published in *Neuropsychoanalysis* (Brown, 2020). Both build upon the more sustained arguments developed within Brown's *Time,* Will and Mental Process (1996) and *Mind and Nature: Essays on* Time and Subjectivity (2000).

DOI: 10.4324/9781003535775-2

1.1 On the Nature of the Present

Jason W. Brown

Introduction

This chapter offers a speculation on the nature of subjective time and the present based on a theory of perception, memory and the mind/brain state. The theory holds that objects generated over a series of antecedent phases terminate in the "mind-external" of the perceived world and perish, with each state revived in the state that follows. An object incorporates a diachronic history that passes from long-term to short-term to iconic memory, with stages or "components" uncovered in forgetting and revival, in the reverse order of their traversal. In a word, the mind/brain state consists in a transition toward an actual object over phases. On this view, forgetting is not trace-decay but an incomplete revival that gradually fades from the near-actual of immediate memory and surface cognition to earlier phases in long-term or experiential memory. The sequence reverses the paradigm of current research.

The claim is that an absolute mental state, that is, a single state isolated from its predecessors – which is an abstraction – consists in the rapid derivation of a whole/part or category/item specification that replicates patterns in morphogenetic sculpting and in evolutionary growth of the forebrain. The transition is a wave of partitions that lead from drive-categories, through the self and conceptual-feeling (desire), to the substrates of imagery (dream, introspection) to object perception (Figure 1.1.1). Phases in the transition are categories (concepts) invested with feeling that partition over segments. The process is a becoming-into-being (Atmanspacher and Filk, 2011) through a qualitative whole/part or fractal-like parsing of categories and their affective tonalities. Feeling in the category is the dynamic of becoming; category is the stability of being. In wakefulness, the process leads to pre-object gestalts that, through the impact of sensibility on the developing configuration, are analysed, externalized and detached as ostensibly mind-independent events.

A single mental state cannot generate a present, however brief, since the revival of prior states within the current state is necessary for the layering on which the present depends. Each mental state actualizes and is revived to a decreasing extent in its successors. Mental states overlap (James, 1890)

DOI: 10.4324/9781003535775-3

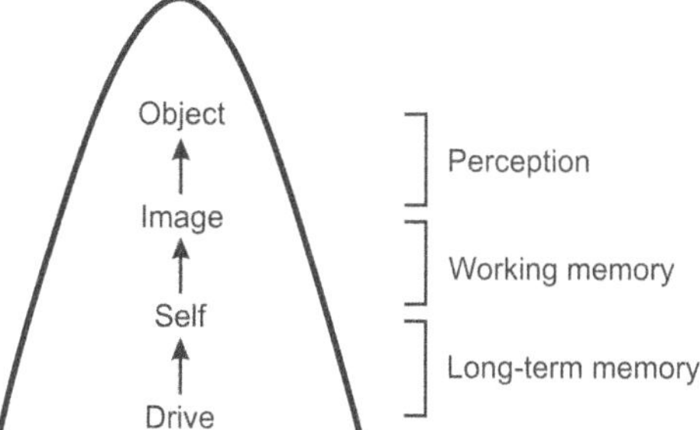

Figure 1.1.1 The mind/brain state begins with drive-categories that pass to the self and desire, to substrates for imagery and dream, to object-representations. The transition is a whole/part or category/member specification. At each phase, categories are invested with feeling. The becoming of the object into being incorporates all phases in the simultaneous epoch of the derivation. The transition is from long-term memory to short-term memory to perception. Incompleteness of revival uncovers stages in memory in the reverse order of the initial traversal.

to create a succession of incomplete revivals over which the state develops. The transition within a state is a before/after succession that begins with instinctual drive and terminates (perishes) as a model of the object world. The succession is ordered and simultaneous until the state actualizes. The simultaneity of succession within a state shifts, on actualization, to the simultaneity of the conscious present, which Whitehead (Whitehead, 1920) defined as "a concrete slab of nature limited by simultaneity". An essential feature of the mental state, as well as other entities, is the epochal nature of the becoming-into-being, which explains the co-occurrence of the self with memorial and perceptual contents in the now.

The category/item transition is analogous to the relation of a duration to its constituents, which are also durations. The relation of whole to part corresponds to that of duration to "instant"; parts are categories with a potential for further partition and instants are durations that can be further individuated. The constituents of durations are virtual, as are category members. A category of animals, or dogs, is inexhaustible; a single dog is a mental category of multiple instantiations. The categorical nature of objects accounts for the identity of Fido over time. Moreover, each instance of specification either actualizes as an endpoint or is a categorical frame for further derivation, just as each stretch of time within a duration is itself a duration.

The Mental State

The mind/brain state (see Chapter 4) is a becoming-into-being that is iterated over phases from drive to acts and objects (Figure 1.1.1). The self-concept develops as a category of potential instantiations accompanied by feeling as desire and its affiliates and derived by partitions from categories (hunger, sexual) of drive (will). There is union *ab origo* of feeling and category. Whitehead (1934) wrote, "...the energetic activity considered in physics is the emotional intensity entertained in life". Isotropic energy is the essence of basic entities; anisotropic feeling is the vitality of organism. Feeling accompanies the object development outward into (as) the world, initially as drive energy, then as desire and the affect in ideas, finally as object worth. The outcome of a transition from drive energy to desire is the value (existence, interest, worth) of objects (see Chapter 5). The self is beneath the posterior boundary or floor of the present. This creates a mental theatre that allows the observer to apprehend subsequent phases – dreams, images, objects – derived from the self and ingredient in the now. Intentionality is in the subjective aim as the trajectory of the conscious self to object and images. Contents in the now – memory images aligned in order of occurrence – descend to a phase of imagery; rather, to the substrates of image-production activated in hallucination and dream that pass to an external world through sensibility at the endpoint of the succession.

The actualization of an epochal whole brings the state into existence with its constituents. The before/after succession is ingredient in the now. Earlier segments form the posterior boundary; object perception forms the anterior boundary. The anterior boundary is fixed by perception, but the posterior boundary, as discussed, is elastic and can include more distant revivals, contracting in dream and certain pathologies when recurrence is limited and the immediate past is unrestored. The posterior boundary, which falls within the range of short-term memory, is replaced by the next most distal revival in the series. Individual states are replaced. The duration of the now is also replaced by overlapping durations. Each recurrence differs mainly in the addition of a proximal phase and the loss of a distal one (Figure 1.1.2).

In the figure, the series A-E represents a sequence of states within present duration, from very recent past states to the immediately present state. Thus, E refers to a completed state of object perception. D refers to preceding states of near-completion (iconic, eidetic memory), while C to A refers to still prior states that show a progressive descent in revival.

With reference to Figures 1.1.2 and 1.1.3, as new perceptions (mental states) arise, they go from the core to long-term memory (LTM) (A) through short-term memory (STM) (B, C) to iconic memory (D) to objects (E). Incomplete revival descends in the reverse order: to iconic, then STM, then LTM. The disparity between A and E – the floor and ceiling of the mental state – which enfolds succession in a stacked simultaneity, is transposed to a longitudinal series as the duration of the now. The stacking is in the order of occurrence. One duration "slides" over another as the earliest or most distal revival sinks below the posterior boundary of the present. In the next mental state, a new anterior boundary appears, such that the succession

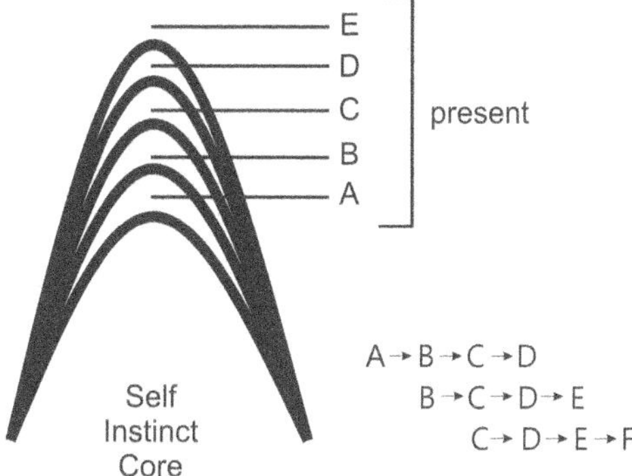

Figure 1.1.2 Time and simultaneity.

incorporates another revival close to the perceptual surface. The present is not a 2D line (Bergson, 1922) but a point in replication, like a window on a changing world.

The dream has been conceived as timeless (von Hartmann, Freud), without a past or future, only a present of limited duration that passes in rapid replacement. The attention of the dreamer is focused on the immediate imagery without recall of prior images or past events. The dream-time resembles in some respects the timelessness of myth in being out of time, with events occurring at multiple times and spaces. The illogic of events that defy common sense and physical laws, as well as having an historic quality relating to the life of the dreamer are also similar to myth. The paradox is that the dream, if timeless, seems to have temporal order. Some claim that dreams begin with ordinary events and culminate in a peak experience; REM studies, which dissociate from dream (Solms, 2000), appear to track the dream in real time. However, even if this is so, it does not refute the fact that dream serializes on waking (see below). How do we resolve the temporal order of the dream narrative with the claim of timelessness? This problem is raised by the extraordinary dream of Maury, as follows:

> Maury, sick in bed, dreamt of the Reign of Terror in the French Revolution, in which he saw horrible bloody scenes and was brought to the courthouse where he saw Robespierre and Marat. He was forced to explain many incidents, was condemned and taken to the place of execution. An immense crowd was there. He climbed the scaffold. The executioner tied him to a table, which flipped as the blade of the guillotine went down. Maury felt his head separated from his body and woke in a panic, realizing that the headboard of the bed crashed on his neck at the same time as the blade of a guillotine.

Freud (1900) struggled with an interpretation of the dream, finally settling on the idea of a pre-packaged story triggered by the headboard. An alternative account, detailed below, is that the succession of dream events is entrained in a simultaneity and achieves temporal order on waking. The headboard that fell on Maury's neck was assimilated to the dream narrative, perhaps retrospectively or only the final episodes. Since the succession was represented simultaneously, that segment closest to the immediate antecedent image would be more malleable than its antecedents (see below).

Memory and Perception

The relation of memory to perception is central to the analysis of dream. In the standard account, recall is divided into components: iconic/echoic and immediate, short-term or working, and long-term with episodic and semantic or procedural and declarative constituents Eidetic or iconic imagery has a pictorial quality that rapidly fades. STM exhibits "physical" attributes of the perceptual object. In LTM, memory is stored, especially its meaning or gist. The perception is presumed to pass from iconic to immediate to STM to LTM. Dream transforms memory, perhaps serving to consolidate certain of the contents of daytime perception. According to the standard model, memory is post-perceptual, recall is retrieval from a file, and forgetting is largely trace-decay. This outline of memory processing, though considerably refined over the years, has not been seriously questioned.

In microgenetic theory, the sequence of stages in memory is reversed. Perception begins with instinctual drive – the animal inheritance – passing to phases that mediate experiential (LTM), then to STM, then to iconic memory. Finally, the forming object is constrained by sensibility to adapt to reality and detach as an independent thing in the world. This means that to some extent we know the object before we consciously perceive it. Merleau-Ponty (1962) wrote, we remember objects into perception. Whitehead (1920) also wrote of perception as vivid remembrance. Thought begins with instinct (Wittgenstein) and passes to the world surface. This conforms to the idea of drive as the core of every act of cognition. Mental states recur in overlapping waves such that, as in microgenetic theory, oncoming states revive their predecessors to a progressively diminished extent. Initial revivals reach the level of iconic (eidetic) imagery, then to phases of STM, and finally fall beneath revival in LTM. The in-processing direction from STM to LTM in standard theory mirrors the sequence, not in the conventional model of perceiving but in forgetting. The disparity between the conscious floor of the state and the perceptual endpoint is transposed to a longitudinal sequence as an epochal duration (Figures 1.1.2 and 1.1.3).

Put differently, the renewal of each state achieves near-perceptual clarity, then, in descent, retains the "physical" features of the object, then descends to LTM and experiential or meaning relations. Memory is pre-perceptual, forgetting and the "components" of memory reflect degree of recurrence, and the trace is the entire process up to the endpoint of revival. On this view, the object is the outcome of a process of actualization in which stages in memory are recapitulated in forgetting in the order of their entrainment in perception.

Dream is an endogenous process, but so is perception. Dream is an object development that does not terminate in a confrontation with incoming sensibility and adaptive sculpting. The transition to a conscious mental state passes from instinctual drive-categories and the liminal self, that is, conceptual primitives laden with drive energy, first hunger, then sexual drive, to conceptual-feeling and desire which, as value, accompanies the pre-object outward to an externalized object (see *From Drive to Value*). Phases that mediate emotion and imagery are transformed into their successors and incorporated in the object formation.

The overlap of states accounts for the proximal embedding of predecessors. Within each state, preceding actualities are revived less and less over time. The present contains incomplete revivals of prior states, until revival sinks below the threshold of LTM where, largely forgotten and inaccessible, it guides, as part of experiential and world knowledge (see *Feeling and Action*), the arousal of each new state. Immediately-prior states are close to the endpoint of perception; those more distant assume an earlier position in the succession.

Figure 1.1.3 shows the overlap of successive states, in which the core of drive, self and experiential knowledge are re-animated prior to the perishing of the state. The overlap revives earlier phases of experiential knowledge, personality and drive. Thus, Tn+1 revives earlier phases in Tn before Tn actualizes. This accounts for the persistence (replication) of earlier phases in subsequent states, while later phases perish to make way for novel perceptions. Overlap explains continuity of states, and the growth of earlier phases of experience, while later phases, close to perception, actualize and perish. The core of personality and character is renewed in oncoming states, while superficial phases that exteriorize as perceptual objects are not revived to completion. The richness, unity and potential of earlier phases, rooted in the accumulation of past mental states, contrasts with the transience and diversity of later ones that lay down the world manifold. This contributes to the disparity between the floor of the mental state in LTM and the ceiling of the state in objectification. This disparity and the depth to which the floor is incorporated in LTM are, as discussed, the bases for the span of duration extracted from the interval between earlier and final converted to a "horizontal" stretch of momentary time enfolding some length of the very recent past. Serialization in the present converts objects to events that can expand through earlier revivals. The disparity creates a temporal illusion – the specious present – analogous to the illusion of a spatial image in binocular disparity.

In sum, the passage of the world is realized in transient bursts of perception that fade in each recurrence. A mental state is added to an epoch of duration as the trailing state dissolves beneath the floor of remembrance. Physical passage is bracketed by the present as novel moments appear. The "moving finger writes ... and moves on", while the present, which seems to move in concert with the world, merely replaces the forward state in a new epoch of duration.

Duration of the Present

How, then, do we go from before/after succession to present duration and perspectival time? Assume a stacking of prior states – incomplete revivals – in the current epoch. The succession is from revivals in the very recent past that progressively recede in the renewal of the next penultimate phase. The before/after succession does not exist in time until it actualizes, at which point segments become contents in conscious duration in the "temporal thickness" of the epochal present. The actualization of an epoch shifts the simultaneity of preliminary segments (fading states) to temporal order in the now. The duration of an epoch (mind/brain state) is estimated at about 0.1 seconds of (clock) time based on "perceptual moment" research (Stroud, 1956). Poppel (1988a, 1988b) argued from Necker cube and duck/rabbit reversals, phrase length in poetry, and other observations that the duration of the present is about 1–2 seconds. If so, this would imply that the present incorporates the revival of 10–20 mind/brain states. Since tones and words are not held in memory but are descending segments of incomplete revivals, the past boundary is elastic and can include a greater portion of what is termed short-term memory.

However, the duration of the present can be greater than two seconds depending on content and whether it is implicit or explicit in the now. Consciousness of a melody is greater than for a series of random tones; consciousness of a sentence is superior to that for a list of unrelated words. In a brilliant paper, Lashley (1951) illustrated this phenomenon with the spoken phrase, "rapid righting with his uninjured hand saved from loss the contents of the capsized canoe". Here, the interpretation depends on retaining the entire sentence in consciousness. This explanation of the present and perspectival time developing out of earlier/later or before/after dispenses with the need for a scanning device, as Lashley postulated.

Does meaning play a role? Not in perceiving a melody. Meaningless phrases, such as "colorless green ideas..." are recalled better than strings of random words. This is so for neologisms such as "twas brillig and the slithy toves did gyre and gimble in the wabe". Possibly, the felicity or relatedness of adjacent states is critical. There are descriptions of memory prodigies who recall over 30 digits in a monotone and over 90 if given rhythmically. This immediate recall – telephone number memory – implies that other factors are involved in the expansion of the now. Meister Eckhart wrote that the goal of meditation was to approximate the individual present to the eternal now of god's mind. Thus, the present may expand to 30 seconds or more in relation to training, attention, content and other factors. If STM extends for this period of time, this would explain why a succession of 10-20 mental states, even 100 or more, revives the "physical" features of the object.

From Before/After to Perspectival Time

Within each state, preceding actualities are revived to a lesser extent over time. The immediately prior states are closer to the endpoint of object perception; those more distant assume an earlier position in the succession. Forgetting is incomplete revival. The concept of trace-decay, which requires the consolidation and stability of a memory, is inconsistent with a processual account of objects or entities as perishing and recurrent. Things recur over their predecessors with greater incompleteness over time. Whitehead (1934) wrote, "each occasion presupposes the antecedent world as active in its own nature". A replacement model differs from a theory of causal progression, in which mental states are conceived as the concatenation of atomic units. In some theories mental states consist of an arising and decay, even an abiding. In sum, the succession in a mental state from drive-categories and long-term or experiential memory through STM to perception uncovers memorial stages in the attenuation of iterated revivals.

Once an epoch actualizes, the temporal order (succession) of the simultaneity becomes conscious, though simultaneity is preserved in duration. Contents in the now can be implicit or explicit. That is, the segments or revived contents of prior states – simultaneous in pre-conscious mind – serialize in the temporal thickness of the present. Figures 1.1.2 and 1.1.3 show segments in the

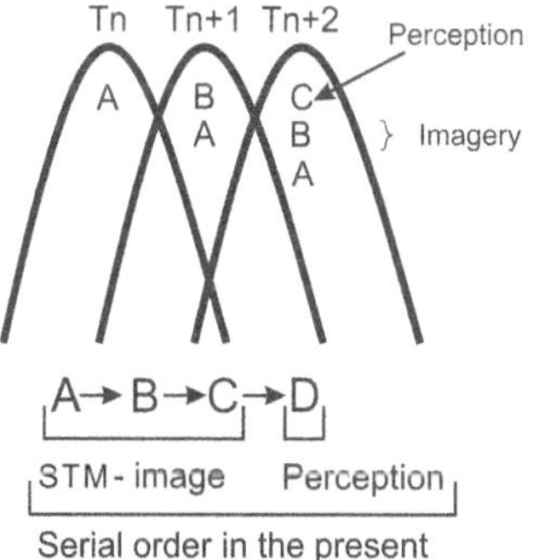

Figure 1.1.3 Overlapping mental states. The state A is revived in the next state, B, then in the ensuing state C. Each state is less completely revived, giving a succession from earlier to later. Revivals within each state fall within segments that mediate mental imagery. Succession within a state is a simultaneity that, on actualization, remains simultaneous but within the conscious time-order of the now. Succession actualizes to conscious serial order in the present (see text).

realization of the state as a "vertical" succession in order of occurrence – the most recent are the most superficial – while the same segments on completion of the state are shown as a "horizontal" series in the now. The before/after that characterizes passage *within* the state becomes, on completion, an event-series in the duration of the now. The simultaneity *within* the state shifts to the simultaneity of conscious time-order. The epochal nature of the mind/brain state becomes the epochal nature of the present; both state and present are simultaneous durations, but contents in the duration of the state are unconscious until actualization, at which point they become conscious in the now.

The duration of the present encloses phases in the immediate past that are relatively superficial in a descent to the liminal self, which represents a floor of recollection. If short-term (or "working") memory retains the "physical" features of the object and extends perhaps 10–30 seconds or so after the object is perceived, contents in the present will occupy a portion of those available to STM. Unlike LTM, in which the gist or meaning of an event is recalled, the images in STM realize physical attributes relating to the original object. Since revivals close to the perceptual endpoint of the state at the anterior boundary of the present are relatively distant from the phase that corresponds to the self, they will approximate the clarity of the occurrent perception. Words in a sentence or tones in a melody embedded in the perception are memory images that retain general features of the object. Revival to the proximal sector of STM accounts for co-occurrence in a brief sequence of words or tones. The serialization of states in present duration converts the immediate object to an event, ordinarily brief but one that can be enlarged by incorporating still earlier revivals. This implies an event-ontology given the abstractness of a single state and the fiction of nature at an instant, and the necessity of a series in which each state enfolds its predecessors.

Music and conversation are auditory perceptions that require duration, but the same process in vision accounts for the perception of change, whether the flight of a bird, a tree shaking in the wind or an image of a mouse crawling over an elephant. The series of mental states in the perception of a stationary object such as a tree is roughly the same with minimal change over the series. With a relatively uniform series in visual perception, the object or object-category is repeated; the category is re-instantiated in similar revivals and the object appears the same. The recurrence of a similar perception in audition gives continuous noise; in visual perception it gives an event-series even if objects appear solid and motionless.

1.2 Time and the Dream

Jason W. Brown

Imagery and the Real

The central phenomenon of dream is primarily the visual or verbal image, though the deaf may dream in sign and cases of cortical blindness may have purely auditory or verbal dreams. The images are commonly vivid, like some hallucinations that are more vivid than waking objects. The content may be banal, fantastic or creative, pleasing or frightening, and there are many anecdotes of problem-solving and creativity in dream and transitional states, from Kekule's benzene ring to the *Kublai Khan* of Coleridge and Wagner's Prelude to *Das Rheingold*, that imply that dreams have meanings in relation to ongoing experience as well as the recall or re-working of prior memories or, for some, as a forecast of things to come.

Dream images rapidly come and go. The image does not have the stability of an object though recurrent dreams are not uncommon. Dream images appear real though they are not object-like in their realness. That is, the feeling of reality in dream, which is due to the lack of one perceptual modality to disconfirm the others – a conspiracy of the senses – is not due to the reality of the image. Similarly, a visual hallucination, say of the face, may seem unreal until it is joined by a verbal hallucination and the face begins to speak, at which point the hallucination is judged to be real. This shows that a judgment of the real is independent of the image on which that judgment is made. Dream images are fleeting, fluid and mutable with unstable boundaries and, like scenic hallucinations, can melt into a space that is foreshortened and lacking in depth, palpable and viscous, not the empty space of waking consciousness. Generally, dream images differ from waking hallucinations in their mobility, meaning-content and entrainment of all perceptual modalities, while hallucinations, though a variety of types, tend to be static, often the face and torso, verbal in psychosis and visual in mescal-induced hallucinations or with posterior brain lesion. The psychotic hears voices while the dreamer has visions. All that we know of dream imagery and its content, its import to the dreamer and the narrative of the dream, is what is retained on waking, usually for

DOI: 10.4324/9781003535775-4

seconds and then mostly forgotten save those dreams that, for one reason or another, are fully recollected and engraved in memory. Jung's lengthy dreams and full recall are unusual in this respect.

There are many forms of imagery, especially in pathological states, all relating to phases in object-formation. The image develops over the same neural pathways as the object; it is an incomplete object. Damage in the visual field can give hallucination in that locus; auditory hallucinations occur during lacunae in auditory perception. Except for after-images, which appear as a film over objects, the hallucinatory image replaces the object-perception. One cannot have a perception and hallucination in the same locus of the visual field or the same time in audition. This does not mean that an object is an externalized hallucination or that an image is embedded in an object; what externalizes is adaptive sculpting by sensation of the pre-object configuration that has traversed phases of potential imagery. This includes memory and thought imagery, auto-symbolic imagery and eidetic imagery close to the perceptual surface, and after-imagery which, by virtue of its physical features, arises at the transition to the world.

Imagery and the Unconscious

Dream is the main, though not only, evidence for unconscious cognition, which some philosophers, notably Searle, have dismissed as mere physiology, though eliminativists would argue the same for waking cognition. There are two issues here: the existence of an unconscious in relation to consciousness, and the occurrence of mental activity that is ordinarily inaccessible to waking mentation. An unconscious inferred from dream might be dismissed as neural firings or as an invention on waking. Arguments for an unconscious, or for unconscious cognition, include a variety of mental phenomena that are not readily explained as constituents of conscious thought, such as irrational, neurotic and psychotic behavior, presuppositions, intuitions, conflicts, core beliefs and values that go into character, compulsions and the impact on the personality of long-forgotten memories. These phenomena cannot be ascribed to waking ideation but are evidence of what is buried in the mind beneath conscious thought. Moreover, consciousness would seem to be essential for an unconscious. It is not likely that unconscious imagery of the type in dream, apart from thought and memory images, occurs during waking perception but rather, that the physiologic substrates of the (potential) image, which are traversed in the realization of an object-perception, exert an influence on the pattern of conscious thought and behavior. This would imply that unconscious activity occurs in waking consciousness but not the imagery of dream, which is released in the absence of external objects, and other occasions of perceptual loss, such as sensory deprivation, snow blindness, hemianopia and so on.

The Self

Though not the self of wakefulness, the experience of a self in dream cannot be doubted. The dream is not an indifferent stream of images that pass without an observer. The dream is my dream and experienced as something that I perceive, that I recall and/or participate in. The pleasure or fear in a dream belongs to me. When someone experiences near-death in a nightmare or a child cries out in panic in a night terror, it is clearly a personal event. However, there are marked differences in the conscious and unconscious self. Unlike the waking self, the self of dream lacks the feeling of agency and is unable to predict or avoid oncoming events, to remember, to effect or resist them, to plan, deliberate, decide, judge, anticipate or regret. There is no analysis of meaning *during* the dream though a dream can be felt as meaningful. Rather, the self is swept along by events without a sharp distinction from the imagery it accompanies nor the opposition, as in waking, of self and object, nor a distinction of inner and outer. The separation of self and image is rudimentary. The brief duration of the dream present, and the lack of objects as a subjective aim, limit the *distance* of self to image. Moreover, the lack of a past in dream, even if the dream itself is memorial, means the self is unsupported by experience or world knowledge and is essentially floating in a truncated mental state. The dream is condensed in an immediate present, with images that have the reality of objects but are not perceived as external and independent of the self. The surfacing of the dream self in psychotic cases may be the basis of paranoia with the self a passive victim to its own imagery.

Recall and Problem-Solving in Dream

Thus, the theory accounts for the accentuation of imagery with an attenuation of final perception and the contraction of present duration, which gives the properties of the dream self. The dominant focus in the dream determines the imagery. Focus on long-term memory (LTM) or experiential memory gives distortions, meaning-relations, affect and relation to personality; focus on short-term memory (STM) and phases close to the object, especially in lucid dreams, gives imagery closer to veridical reality. The onset of each state in instinctual drive and the transition to need and wish conform to principles of interpretation in dream-analysis. The overlap gives continuity, self-identity and the relation to an experiential core. Perishing at objectification, like Freud's magic writing pad analogy, allows for fresh perceptions and severs the link of object to psyche.

Dream is not timeless. Succession is preserved in simultaneity with possible revision on waking. This helps to explain the dream of Maury and similar dreams, such as hearing church bells integrated into a dream narrative when the alarm clock rings. One reason why many dreams have the quality of a series of loosely connected images is that waking states are constrained by changing perceptions, while dream constraints consist largely of the derivations of drive and desire and the foundations of personal experience.

Commonly, on waking from a dream there is a moment when the dreamer apprehends the dream as a whole. Attempts to recall events usually result in forgetting. This can be explained by the revival to iconic or "sensory" memory, which shares the same features, namely a glimpse of the entirety and a loss of the whole on selection of elements. Thus, in experimental studies, if a subject is very briefly shown a matrix of ten letters, there is momentary recall of the whole. Asked to recall a vertical or horizontal column, the subject may recall the column requested but other letters fade away. Similarly, the revival of dream to the phase of iconic memory immediately on waking, which explains a grasp of the whole, is rapidly replaced by object-perceptions. Initially, the entire dream is available, all at once, with clarity but ensuing revivals trigger interference and discontinuity by replacing images with objects. Conversely, occasional dreams recalled in detail may represent a more complete realization at superficial phases.

As to problem-solving, dream-content often consists of day-residues, perhaps the least-noticed, such that meaning-relations can lead to solutions on waking. A personal example. The question of whether dreams involve the most recent brain structures, suggested by the lack of visualization in cortical blindness, was a problem of interest but on which I had no certain opinion. Then, I had a dream in which there was joking in a courtroom of the rhyming of docket money and pocket money. This appeared to be evidence of involvement of left hemisphere language areas that mediate rhyme and phonology. Semantics or word-meaning relations, are less localized in brain. I have also had theoretical difficulties resolved in the auto-symbolic images of Silberer (1951), visual, vivid and creative, in the transitional state, that fuse several lines of thought from the preceding day. Einstein said he thought in visual images. Could a conversion of verbal problems in waking thought to a visual modality in dream reframe problems to allow a substitution that opens a new path to understanding?

Part 2

Subjectivity

Introduction to Section 2: Subjectivity

Paul Stenner

Subjectivity, to Brown's way of thinking, is not to be understood as something mysteriously unique to human beings. Any understanding of humanity requires an account of what might be called the *amplified* nature of human subjective experience compared to what we can assume to be that of other creatures. No other creature has proved as capable of such disastrous philosophical errors, or of such epoch defining hubris, hope, beauty and cruelty, as human beings. Comparatively speaking, human modes of thought, imagination, reminiscence, agency and self-consciousness are the seed-ground of outrageous novelty. Brown's premise is that the common ingredient of all subjectivity is a subject capable of distinguishing inner phenomena from outer events. Indeed, this capacity to distinguish inner phenomena and outer events can be viewed as the constitutive paradox of subjectivity.

The first chapter in this second section (2.1) is based on an article first published in *The Journal of Mind and Behavior* (Brown, 2020). It takes as its problem the animal origins of human subjective experience. The starting point is that animal subjectivity is most characterised by objectivity. Mind is inseparable from the biosphere of the animal's *Umwelt:* glued, as it were, to external happenings, with inner phenomena at a minimum. Brown outlines the key mechanisms through which human subjectivity has achieved a degree of flexible contingency compared to this high animal standard, buying, as it were, a greater degree of interiority at the cost of expanding the potential for error concerning the external. It is here that Brown develops the important arguments about neoteny noted in Stenner's introductory essay.

The second chapter (2.2) outlines the nature of the mind/brain state and is based on an article published in *The Journal of Mind and Behavior* a year later than the first (Brown, 2021). Here, Brown shows how his conception of the mind/brain state allows a novel resolution to the usual impasse between those who resolve the paradox of subjectivity by reduction toward the objective (the mind is in the world) and those who do so by reduction toward the subjective (the world is in the mind).

DOI: 10.4324/9781003535775-5

2.1 Origins of Subjective Experience

Jason W. Brown

Introduction

In this chapter, we will describe processes involved in the evolution of subjective experience and the shift from animal to human mind. The question is, how can one explain the appearance of mental phenomena, such as the self, thought and imagery and consciousness of inner events and objects in relation to a theory of the mind/brain state, as well as evolutionary and developmental processes that are responsible for this enormous leap in mental capacity. A description of the mental state has appeared elsewhere (chapter *From Drive to Value*), while processes that account for cognitive advance have been previously discussed in relation to a theory of symptoms or errors with focal brain lesions, though the theory has not addressed, except by inference, the relation of pathology to normal cognition. It turns out that the same processes that account for pathology also account for further development. The theory has focused on two epigenetic mechanisms, parcellation (Changeux, 1985; Ebbeson, 1984) and heterochrony (Goodwin, 1982), with particular attention to neoteny (Gould, 1982). The one accounts for pattern, the other timing. First, an account of errors in language, then an account of the relation of error to mental process.

The Nature of the Error

Since neuropsychology shifted from a qualitative description of symptoms to a quantitative measure of performance, the error has been viewed as anecdotal, non-repeatable and without scientific value, displaced by an interpretation of scores on various tests or probes while the error, which was of primary interest in the past, has fallen into disregard. This is partly because of the effort to turn psychology into a quantitative science, and partly for lack of an interpretation of the error as something other than a guess. Take a common language error, misnaming as an example, say a patient with aphasia and left posterior brain damage who names a chair as a table. Clearly, the error points to a category of furniture in which a word related in the category is selected. It should be noted

DOI: 10.4324/9781003535775-6

that such within-category errors are the rule in pathological cases. Patients will name red as blue, not as a chair, or identify a face as another person, not a hat. Prior accounts of error, none successful, have proposed an equalization of associative strength (Pavlov), a reversion to an earlier stage (regression hypothesis), a shift from abstract to concrete attitude (Goldstein) and inhibition, dis-inhibition, release or compensation by neighboring or contralateral regions in the brain (e. g., diaschisis; von Monakow, 1914).

My interpretation many years ago was that focal brain injury exposed normal preliminary phases in a recurring process in the realization of an act of language or cognition, but a more precise formulation was not forthcoming at the time. This situation changed with the publication of studies on epigenetic mechanisms that conformed to microgenetic theory, and opened the door to an account of errors from an ontogenetic standpoint. Previously, the problem with an ontogenetic correlation was that the brain develops more or less as a whole over a span of years, unlike phylogeny which has millions of years to lay down formative structure, so a correlation of brain region and developmental stage is not a simple matter.

The finding of a relation of growth to dynamic process in brain was in stark contrast to the still-dominant view of encapsulated or modular functions in a brain conceived as a static circuit board. These studies were evidence that fetal and post-natal growth (morphogenesis) appeared to be of great relevance to understanding the nature of the error. Specifically, while prior accounts of ontogeny in relation to symptoms of brain pathology emphasized a regression back through stages in acquisition – an unpeeling of the onion-skin of development – epigenetic studies led to the idea of a continuation of brain-developmental process into later life. This suggests that pathology is not related to stages in acquisition but uncovers processes in early growth that account for normal mentation. The implication is that the *timing* and *pattern* of brain process in development plays a role in mental process in the adult, uniting microgenesis and ontogenesis. The concept of a regression can be replaced by the observation, through the effect of focal disruption, that pathology uncovers processes relating to growth trends in development. In a word, the underlying process is exposed, not the behavior that the process lays down.

The first "mechanism" to consider is neoteny, a selective slowing or retardation of a juvenile stage in development and its prolongation into later structure or function. Gould (1982) illustrated the effect by citing older work comparing the human form to a "fetal ape," indicating that a prolongation of a fetal stage could account for evolutionary advance (Somel et al., 2009). Neoteny can lead to birth anomalies or to greater development. One example is the prolonged period of childhood dependency and delayed sexual maturity in humans compared to apes. However, the most striking example is the prolongation of a fetal stage of rapid brain growth well into the post-natal period that accounts for the great increase in brain size. Along with this, another neotenous feature, postponement in the closure of the cranial sutures, allows for expansion of the skull after birth to accommodate a larger brain which otherwise would not pass through the pelvic canal.

If we consider that a focal lesion does not, as is widely assumed, degrade or destroy a brain area or a function but disrupts the flow in a wave-front, with the effect of a delay in the process mediated by the damaged area, the significance of the symptom takes on a new light. We can assume from studies of a variety of aphasic errors that the process of word-finding proceeds from fields of wide to narrow semantic distance, with a progressive zeroing in on the target category and word. This is also true for phonology, with some errors reflecting a distance of several phonological features and others only one. This would mean that the specification of a lexical item is delayed at a phase prior to elicitation, namely, as in the above example, the category of furniture, such that either the word chair or table could individuate. In fact, if the correct word *chair* is produced, it has more expansive (holophrastic) semantic boundaries than in the normal individual, and can be used for stool, bench and so on, much as the word daddy in infants applies to all men, or doggy to animals. Overinclusion of semantic boundaries has been shown in aphasics with posterior brain damage.

The interpretation is that retardation, or neoteny, prolongs the phase of specification in a semantic category, at times leading to a correct response or to one of related meaning. If neotenous prolongation affects the substrates of phonology, the required word *table*, might be pronounced as a word like *dabel*, a phonemic error close to the target, or a neologism such as *catal*, where the distance from target is more pronounced. The error reflects the degree of individuation within the phonemic category, but the specification-effect is the same, zeroing down on the final phoneme. These principles apply to all domains of cognition (Somel, Tang, and Khaitovich, 2012), not just language, for example, the appearance of illusion or hallucination as a pre-perceptual phase with damage to visual cortex. A last point is that neoteny is not a block or ceiling on the process which, though delayed, continues on to the ensuing phase. Thus an incorrect word still undergoes normal phonological realization at a subsequent phase. In the same way, brain size eventually reaches equilibrium and the cranial sutures close.

Epigenesis and Cognitive Process

The concept of neoteny applied to process in a momentary act of cognition – the mind/brain state – and the revival of the effect over successive states, allows us to reconstruct from errors the normal sequence of events underlying word-production and, by implication, all other mental functions. It also has the advantage of understanding the brain as an organic system in dynamic flux in which patterns of growth, of mental process and disruptions in normal flow all have a common basis. This epigenetic mechanism is also to be considered in relation to arguments by Goodwin (1982), that morphogenesis, conceived as a 4-D process in time, can be viewed as first laying down form in the form of structure, and then, with a more or less completed morphology, laying down form in the form of process. In other words, the morphology does not output functions; rather, a process of growth lays down morphology and continues as a mental process that underlies cognition. Specifically, mind/brain process develops as a prolongation of morphogenetic growth trends. From this it is evident that neoteny, at least in part, is responsible for the advance from animal mind to human mind. The errors in language and cognition are explained by neotenous delay of process in the mental state, and that mental process is a continuation of epigenetic trends in fetal growth.

Parcellation

While neoteny can account for the relation of symptom to focal brain damage in a dynamic model of brain activity, another mechanism is required to account for the process of progressive specification. For this we look again to morphogenesis and the process of sculpting or parcellation in fetal brain growth. The fundamental principle that underlies parcellation is an exuberant production of cells and connections in fetal brain, and an elimination of redundancy that gives specificity in connections (Schaefer, Kong, and Yeo, 2016). The implication is that growth and learning primarily accompany a loss of cells and connections. This can reach astonishing levels. It has been estimated that in macaque monkey at time of sexual maturity there is a loss of over two trillion synapses.

I have suggested that what begins in morphogenesis as elimination of cells and connections continues after a relatively stable morphology in the inhibition of alternate routes of cognitive process to arrive at a specificity of outcome. Put differently, elimination is replaced by inhibition as the vehicle of specification. Thus, visual potentials recorded over a wide distance in juveniles are gradually restricted to visual cortex. There is evidence of diffuse organization of the hemispheres early in life (Semmes, 1968) with specification of the left side for language processes. Cerebral dominance can be explained in this way as well. The most dramatic example is sculpting of endogenous gestalts by sensibility at the endpoint of the perceptual process (see below, Figure 2.1.1). The implication of these findings is that what begins as a competitive pruning of redundancy in early brain growth continues with inhibition as the basis of focality in the maturing brain to become the pattern of cognitive process. Content undergoes progressive individuation leading from generality to concision through a cascade of whole/part or category/member shifts in the passage over levels in the mental state.

To apply this to the prior discussion of aphasia, the process of zeroing in on a target reflects the suppression or falling aside of other potential alternatives. The progression is from wide to narrow category relations leading to the final word, act or object. Mental process is selection by inhibition of competing possibilities. Every thought or object represents that which is left after other potential options have been eliminated. The microgenetic parsing of configurations over phases in the mental state is analogous to sculpting in the development of morphology in ontogenesis. Moreover, the fractionation of mental content through elimination of alternatives conforms to evolutionary selection by the elimination of unfit exemplars. There is continuation of a growth pattern from evolution (survival of the fittest), to morphogenesis (parcellation or sculpting) to a whole-to-part transition in the mental state (progressive individuation), confirming a common growth process over different time scales: millions of years in evolution, a lifespan in maturation and a fraction of a second in microgenesis.

Subjective Experience

Mental content applies *inter alia* to self, consciousness, thought, reminiscence, agency and imagery. Verbal imagery refers to inner speech; visual imagery to the visual imagination, including spatial thought, symbolism and dreams. The common ingredient in all states is a self that is conscious of inner phenomena and outer events, and the distinction between them. There can be states of mental vacancy but, generally, objects are essential, in actuality or in memory, for a waking self to be conscious of inner content. In the absence of perception, consciousness is rudimentary, as in dream and the self is passive to a stream of images. In animals, there is absolute objectivity. The mind of an animal is inseparable from the biosphere in which it lives. Animal mind fully objectifies without, so far as we know, an interior portion, such that the organism is part of what it observes. The absence of subjective content deprives the organism of an interior life, so that it is perpetually glued to external happenings. Behavior is driven by non-conscious instinct and the changing environment without a self to anchor a state of awareness or an experience of "I see that" or "I feel this." The first hints of interior content occur in the higher mammals, especially primates, when the animal shows an interest or curiosity in objects that do not necessitate immediate action.

What is proposed here is that the appearance of mental events in the context of an object perception, or the completion of a state of object-formation, is explained by a neotenous delay of segments in the mental state that ordinarily undergo rapid transit and remain tacit or inchoate in the object. These segments, which are the substrates of self and imagery, are prolonged to give rise to mental phenomena. Specifically, a focal delay in the transit of preperceptual substrates of potential imagery evokes imaginal content – verbal, visual, etc. – to emerge in the abeyance of external objects. In this respect, the partition of submerged potential to imagery resembles the lesion-induced prolongation of phases in language that reveal processes that are ordinarily concealed from observation. The categories that specify images correspond with those that specify words. The prolongation can be viewed as a focal neoteny within and over a series of states. The conceptual source of the image that was implicit in perception now comes to the fore as explicit content. Passage continues to objects but the world recedes to the background with the prominence of mental content. In thinking, an arousal of the experiential and world knowledge that are embedded in the object arise in the delayed termination of that phase. Along with this, the lack of complete specification to an object leads to an indefiniteness – the basis of uncertainty and choice in thinking – in the content that emerges. Indefiniteness is the conceptual analog of parcellation in growth in that thought entails possibility prior to the final datum.

The arousal of a self at the liminal boundary of the mental state is fundamental and essential to the occurrence of all other contents. The self is aroused in relation to drive-based feeling prior to imagery. First, a proto-self is aware of objects; then, mental events arise for the self to be conscious of (Figure 2.1.1). Neoteny provides an explanation for the emergence of mental phenomena which, as in morphogenesis, accompany a lack of complete individuation. Sculpting of the final object achieves full specification. Preperceptual content is incompletely specified. This lack of specification is the basis of choice and decision-making, namely, that contents in mind do not fractionate to the same degree as objects. The indecision occasioned by lack of resolution can involve everyday choices or the most profound in life, from a decision on dinner or a film to the "to be or not to be" of life or death.

In directed thought there is a subjective aim toward a specific outcome. The outcome is largely shaped by pragmatic values. Thought is adaptive but, unlike the final perception, it lacks specificity and the process can be derailed. Imagery that arises still earlier, as in dream, is closer to meaning and past experience. The self lacks agency and is receptive to the flow of images. Goethe wrote of a descent to the pool of the creative unconscious. The greater the depth, the more pronounced the novelty and/or distortion. Conversely, the more superficial the image, as in rational thought or lucid dream, the closer to perceived reality. The elicitation of self and mental content depends on the dominant locus of delay in the mental state, closer to drive or closer to perception. In either case, novelty elicited in neoteny prevails over incompleteness in parcellation. What is most remarkable is the economy of these "mechanisms" that are instrumental in the growth of form. Essentially the same processes are involved in evolution as in development and the mind/brain state: process over millions of years, development over the lifespan and actualization in a fraction of a second. In sum, the cognitive process is a process of growth.

Figure 2.1.1 In animal mind, the mental state proceeds from instinctual drive to objects. In apes and young children there is a proto-self in relation to awareness of drive and primitive feelings (Van Essen et al., 2019). Later, the self is conscious of images in the context of an object perception (see text).

Consciousness

The relation of self to mental events is linked to the emergence of consciousness, which is a relation of a self to objects, images and feelings. Initially, a proto-self early in the mental state, is conscious of objects, feelings and needs. This stage gives way to a self in relation to waking mental phenomena such as thought and refined feeling or affect-idea. Neotenous change occurs early, evoking the proto-self as a coalescence of drive; then, at a later phase, the conscious self, the I, appears in relation to waking imagery. There is relative unity of the mental core in the specification of drive, but instinctual displacement occurs and the organism still has a conflict between aggression or defense. There may be hesitation in animals when the drive has not individuated to action. Indecision prior to selection in thought is comparable to the sculpting of redundancy in development. The later appearance of conscious imagery conforms to the description by Vygotsky (1962) of the development of inner speech out of earlier egocentric speech in children, particularly when there is an obstruction or the child is uncertain. The shift from immediacy to indecision – incompleteness of individuation – is the beginning of conscious thought. Immediacy entails an absence of doubt. The uncertainty that accompanies pre-perceptual delay is an ingredient in deliberation and imagination. In a word, the arousal of thought through neotenous prolongation entails some degree of indecision that is analogous to parcellation and incomplete resolution.

This account has implications for our understanding of consciousness, which is not so much a thing to be explained or a problem to be solved as a relation across ingredients. Consciousness is not independent of self and object, which are sufficient for a state of consciousness. The awareness described in animals and young children (Piaget, 1969) is that of a proto-self in relation to objects and activity. Subsequently, a self (I) appears at a supra-liminal phase that self-consciously perceives objects and mental contents. In a state of introspection with inattention to the external, a prolongation of pre-perceptual phases expands the mental state with the effect of greater duration of the present, much as occurs in meditation. More generally, having a self means being conscious, being conscious means having a self to be conscious of something, and having mental experience is what the reflective self is conscious of. In a word, consciousness is the confrontation of a self with its own internal and external images.

2.2 The Mind/Brain State

Jason W. Brown

Introduction

Is the mind an imprint of the world, a tabula rasa to be articulated by experience, as common sense and much of empirical science would have it? Is perceptual reality an elaboration of the mind, as philosophers before and especially after Descartes have maintained, or are there two parallel worlds, inner and outer, in constant interaction? The mind assimilates the world as it shapes experience, adding interest, value, beauty and meaning to a world unpossessed of these qualities. Is the innate constrained or is knowledge instilled? Regardless of which perspective one takes, or the variation on that perspective, the primacy of the self, the evanescence and insubstantiality of thought and the felt unity of mind must be reconciled with the dazzling multiplicity of nature and a solid persisting world. The seemingly insurmountable problem in resolving these perspectives, at least by force of argumentation, which arise from our ignorance of the relation of mind-internal to the outer world, has inspired much of the discussion in philosophy of mind, as well as having an impact on methods of psychological study.

The problem for subjectivism is a world of appearance, of external diversity and mind-independent objects, while for objectivism it is the mentality that underlies behavior – specifically, the self, thought, feeling, consciousness and degrees of the innate – or the contrast of necessity and freedom, of causal nature with a capriciousness of thought and emotion, and the dependence of mind on an impersonal world of certain fact. Science filters individual mind through a community of belief, such that the picture of the world that is built up piecemeal one brick at a time overrides the claims of any one observer. Consensual fact erodes the value of private experience. The goal of empiricism is an aggregate of isolated or local models that sums to a coherent system of explanation, beginning with the world of objects and, derivatively, accounting for the mind in terms of physical brain function.

Toward this end, a common strategy is to transpose the constituents of the world inward to the mind/brain such that the texture of an externalism prevails within the mind itself; for example, the presumption that the lines,

DOI: 10.4324/9781003535775-7

angles, movement and color of perceived objects are recognized by brain receptors – feature detectors which enables an assemblage of those properties to a completed perception. The input of sense data is conceived to combine to form external objects, finessing the question of "projection" of image to object, and replacing internal relations with external connections, as well as avoiding problems of duration and change, not to mention the evolutionary growth and resultant infrastructure through which mind unfolds. The extreme case is an elimination of mental properties altogether in the expectation that future neuroscience will fill in the gaps.

On the other hand, those for whom introspection and the intra-psychic are dispositive seize upon irregularities such as illusions, constancies, dreams and memories to accentuate the priority of mind, or they appeal to quantum effects to reinforce the primacy of mind and consciousness and the commonalty of mind and nature. An emphasis on behavioral or third person data in externalism leaves out the richness of meaning, value and self-realization that are the foundations of life's concerns, while subjectivism has the obligation to explain the relation of mind to a putatively causal nature.

As noted, one casualty of the debate owing to empirical trends in contemporary thought is the description of mental content in terms of logical solids or atomic units, thus mirroring, in mind, the account of external objects. The population of mind by solid non-temporal entities – modules, computational networks – is central to an externalist account of the mind/brain state, for on this view a state can be defined by its (conscious) content, say a belief, a proposition, an after-image, a "raw feel" or quale, permitting a conformance with locality in space and instantaneity in time of entities in mind and world. If mind is constituted by the same atomic units as described in nature, it is possible to identify shared mental states across individuals with the same content; that is, different people who share the same thought can be said to be in the same mental state. Here, relations are recast as connections and the mental state is taken to consist in the isolation of decontextualized contents. To date, the tepid response to this preposterous claim is the inability of externalism to describe the inner feeling of "what it's like" to be a mind; that is, the quality of personal experience that eludes descriptions of behavior (cf. Nagel, 2012). However, an argument as to the impenetrability, except to the individual, of strictly interior content misses the mark. It is not merely the experience of qualia. The world itself should be the field of battle.

In my view, the resolution lies in an adequate theory of what constitutes a mind/brain state that is based on the study of mind and brain independent of a speculative metaphysics, whether from an internal or external standpoint. To anticipate, such a theory should, minimally, address the micro–temporal structure, actualization and replacement of states, the transition through unconscious layers to acts and objects, the conscious self and the duration of the present, as well as the neural processes through which the state is realized. Such an account would also address the relation of mental states to a perceptual world; specifically, the assumed transition of sensibility into mind and the formation of the world through the mental state. This shift, which is generally conceived as an abrupt dissociation, is reconceived as a continuum from mind to world, such that an endogenous configuration is sculpted to a model of reality by extrinsic sense data. With such a model, competing accounts could be re-aligned in accordance with processes through which the mind/brain state actually develops.

Time and Memory

Wittgenstein wrote, and psychoanalysts would agree, as would I, that a mental state begins with instinct as the *animal inheritance* traverses the evolutionary core of the brain. Strands of the inherited and acquired constitute the core self, the "me," which is bound up with bodily function, immediacy and the largely innate determinants of behavior. This construct passes a liminal threshold leading to a conscious self in relation to desire for objects or conditions in the future. The self appears early in the mental state prior to thought and the endpoint of object-perception. A mental state enfolds a transition from instinct to thought to perception in a fraction of a second. Every act, object, and utterance has a brief diachronic history. Conscious experience is recollection adapted by sensation to a model of the real, each occasion presupposing the antecedent world as active in its formation. States recur in overlapping waves, such that oncoming states revive their predecessors to a progressively diminished extent (Figure 2.2.1).

The felt continuity of contiguous mental states is created out of simultaneity with the interstices between states collapsed in the overlap. The succession, enfolded in the present, unpeels in the order of occurrence, with the leading edge of the current state trailed by descending revivals. These incomplete revivals, implicit in the present or as conscious memories, are stacked within the ongoing state and transposed to what feels like a horizontal series in time. The transition from the simultaneity of the state-series to its longitudinal unfolding occurs in a phenomenal present in which the most recent state replaces its predecessor and the most distant state falls beneath remembrance.

In Figure 2.2.1, state A is replaced by B, B by C, and so on. D is the forward edge of the perception; A is the trailing one that slips beneath recall. The disparity between D and A is present duration. The stacking of recurrent and fading states is in the order of occurrence. One duration replaces another as the earliest or most distal revival sinks below the posterior boundary of the present. In each ensuing state, a new anterior boundary appears, such that the succession incorporates another revival close to the perceptual surface. Duration is epochal, not divisible to instants. The simultaneity within and across mental states aligns with the event-series that accumulates over a "length" of physical time. The simultaneity of the series – a temporal thickness from the recent past to the forward edge of perceptual immediacy – actualizes perspectival time

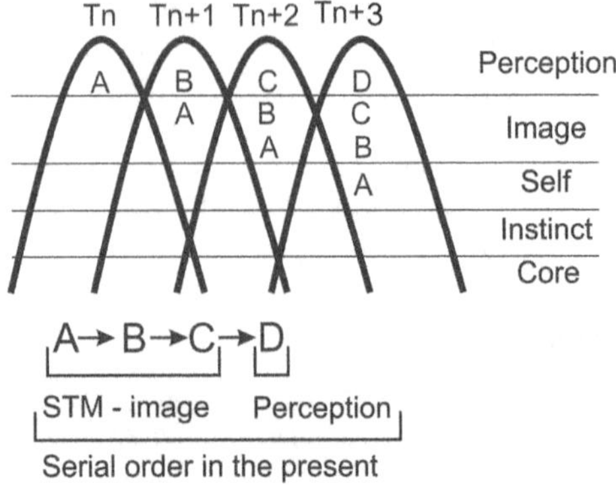

Figure 2.2.1 Successive states are embedded in the present state as incomplete revivals. The states are "stacked" in order of occurrence, but are simultaneous until the state actualizes and an epochal duration is achieved. That is, the actualization constitutes an epochal whole but is experienced as serial order in the present. The revival sinks to iconic, then short-term (STM), then long-term memory, the reverse of the original perception. The overlap of states affects only the earlier segments. This accounts for the re-instantiation of early segments of instinctual drive, knowledge, character and core values. These refer to preliminary phases in the mental state, while distal phases corresponding to final objects are not overlapped and perish to allow for novel perceptions (see text).

with past and future felt within the present moment. The past can be revived as the dominant segment in the sequence. Segments in the realization of the state are shown as a "vertical" succession in order of occurrence – the most recent are the most superficial – while the same segments, on completion of the state, are overlapping and experienced as a longitudinal series. The earlier to later transition from core to endpoint – the becoming of an epoch – creates the duration essential for a perspectival now.

The transition from the instinctual and unconscious passes through the arousal of mental contents that reflect a conceptual and an affective complement. In human mind, the transition from self to objects gives consciousness of the world. With an arousal of segments midway in the mental state, there is consciousness of thoughts and feelings in the context of object–awareness. In dream, the pre-perceptual phase of imagery becomes more pronounced, and distorted, with the elimination of objects.

This differs completely from the standard account, in which recall is divided into components: iconic/echoic and immediate, short-term or working memory, and long-term memory (LTM) with a distinction between episodic and semantic or procedural and declarative. Eidetic or iconic imagery has a pictorial quality that rapidly fades. Short-term memory exhibits "physical" attributes of the perceptual object. In LTM, memory is stored, especially its

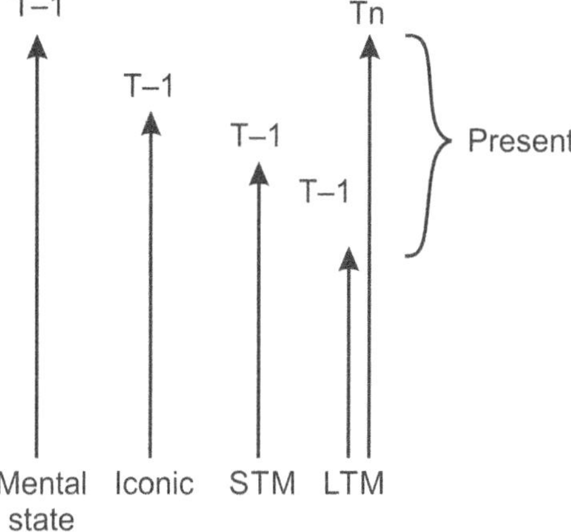

Figure 2.2.2 The mental state at T–1 is a transition from drive to self through imagery or its substrates to the object world. The state recedes in successive revivals, first to iconic recall, then short-term memory, then long-term memory, finally beneath the floor of recollection. Revival of states traverses the same phases as in the original perception. Put differently, forgetting uncovers the sequence of phases in perception. The present is extracted from the disparity between the perceptual surface and the floor of remembrance. In this model, the transition from drive to object in the mental state is that of earlier to later in physical time, while the present is an illusory span over the simultaneity of a succession of states that accounts for subjective or perspectival time.

meaning or gist. The perception is *presumed* to pass from iconic to immediate memory, to short-term memory, to LTM, from a physiological stage to consolidation and storage. Dream is a transform of memory, perhaps serving to consolidate certain of the contents of daytime perception. However, commonly it is the least-noticed fragments that recur, which may run counter to the concept of consolidation. According to this model, memory is post-perceptual, recall is retrieval from a file, and forgetting is due to interference and trace decay. This outline of memory processing, though considerably refined over the years, has not been seriously questioned. Microgenetic theory (Figure 2.2.2) reverses the conventional account, such that the same sequence in perception occurs in forgetting and recall.

Drive

The fundamental shift in the origin of drive is from the circularity of reflex (Weizsaecker, 1939/1958) to a co-temporal act–object. The reflex is a self-contained concatenation of stimulus–response (S-R) or causal pairs where a stimulus elicits a response that serves as a stimulus for another S-R reaction. The organism achieves freedom from the circularity and inevitability of reflex by a co-incident arousal of act and object. The initial phase is a transition from reflex to representation (Figure 2.2.3). The developing act and object, liberated from the seriality of reflex, undergo a synchronous transition over a succession of phases in the mental state.

In this shift, small (internuncial) brainstem cells intercalated between the limbs of a reflex arc, which form a pool from which a simultaneous act/object arises, may be the decisive factor. The construct arising from this kernel of cells is presumed to constitute parallel systems for action and perception – endogenous, hierarchic – surrounded by extrinsic multi-tiered systems for sensibility – successive constraints on percept-formation – and physical keyboards for motor discharge. Intermediate phases are substrates in the realization of acts and objects, or they are aroused as intra-psychic content – emotions and concepts – in the context of a completed object-perception. The supposition is that act and object arise from a common midline source, with feelings and concepts as intermediate phases in the course of actualization. A model for the unified act/object is the optic grasp of a frog catching a fly, in which the target is seen at the same moment the tongue darts out. The concept of an action system stratified over the neuraxis in

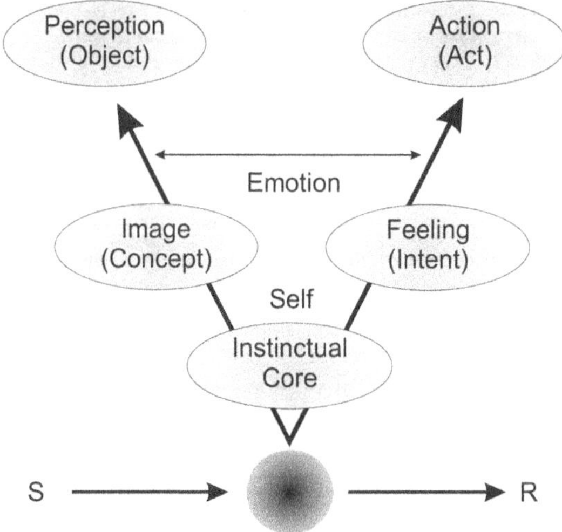

Figure 2.2.3 Acts and objects develop in parallel out of an instinctual core, traversing substrates of imagery and emotion. The percept-development transports drive-categories through concepts to objects. The act-development transports drive-impulse through feeling to acts. Concepts give the quality of emotion. Feeling gives the intensity.

evolutionary layers from ancient to recent was postulated by Yakovlev (1948) and extended by Bernstein (1967).

Parenthetically, I proposed the same organization for the posterior and anterior systems in language; that is, a temporal–parietal system for word formation and perception, and a frontal system for grammar and articulation, with connections between them for synchronization at successive phases. Transcortical connections serve to keep the systems in phase. An utterance is the outcome of a parallel realization of act and object development, not a transmission from a posterior to anterior system. The anterior or action component develops out of rhythmic levels that lay down the prosodic or intonation pattern, the posterior perceptual component is derived through lexical concepts. The process leads to a phonetic (anterior) and phonemic (posterior) endpoint. Speech has its onset in breath groups linked to respiratory timing arising at a depth of process. In contrast, concepts are frames of potential pre-perceptual images that actualize in objects.

Part 3

Thought and Value

Introduction to Section 3: Thought and Value

Paul Stenner

As is implicit when we distinguish value-judgements from truth-judgements, issues of value, feeling and belief are often treated as extrinsic to the world of nature itself. It is as if they were projected by the machinery of the mind, for the questionable benefit of a spectator subject, onto the screen of nature: itself blankly neutral about the matter of whether and how these things matter. Particularly if physics is taken as the standard, the task of producing a homogeneous account of nature is greatly simplified if matters of value, feeling and belief are treated in this way as human, all too human, projections. Process thought, by contrast, has long taken inspiration from the life sciences, including Darwin's actual preoccupations with the theatre of agency amongst living organisms. This perspective makes it harder to ignore valuation as an intrinsic feature of nature. When psychological science arrives on the scene, one might think that it becomes impossible to evade the question as to whether value is intrinsic to nature or an extrinsic projection of mind. But actually, lack of clarity is still common. Most academic forays into value, as Brown points out, concentrate attention on the nature of the object of value (a good act, a work of art) while saying little about the valuation of the object as a process in its own right.

When Brown addresses value in the first chapter of this third section (Chapter 3.1), he makes clear that his interest is in value *creation.* This is a question of the *origination* of value in the mind *and hence* (given mind is part of the world) in world. This chapter is based on an article in *Process Studies* (Brown and Zhadiaiev, 2022). Brown finds the roots of value even in the roots of plants, where tropism fits his definition of 'preference' as the *selection* of one thing or direction over another. This is not to assume, of course, that the plant is conscious of its preference in the way that humans (sometimes) are when we value. The chapter is self-consciously speculative. It proposes the emergence of value as the issue of a sequence that moves from drive through emotion to desire. Each phase in the sequence is internally complex. Hence,

DOI: 10.4324/9781003535775-8

in Brown's account, emotion is the fusion of feeling (supplying emotional intensity) and concept (supplying emotional quality), each of these being part of distinguishable unfolding trajectories of becoming: feelings issuing from drive energy and giving rise to actions; concepts issuing from drive categories and giving rise to objects. Hence, the premature interruption of an object-in-formation reveals a concept (or image), while the pre-terminal segment of an action is a feeling.

The next chapter (Chapter 3.2) takes forward this distinction between the conjoint becomings of actions and objects to focus in on the problem of 'feeling and action'. It offers a reinterpretation of a series of concepts fundamental to action theory, including volition, agency and choice, self and decision, intent, and freedom.

The final chapter (Chapter 3.3) broaches the problem of 'thought and belief'. Refreshingly, Brown steers clear both of weighty philosophical debates and of the intricacies of psychological models of perception and memory. Instead, he provides an overview of a collection of 'cognitive' processes starting with perception and moving on to belief, certainty and conviction, delusion and knowledge before concluding with a section on memory and truth. He makes the case that, notwithstanding the culturally and consciously refined complexity found in human exemplifications of each of these processes, they are nevertheless rooted in drive energy and categories common, in some way, shape or form, to all life. The ideal aim of cognition is the individuation, within the medium of conceptual feeling, of objects for action.

3.1 From Drive to Value

Jason W. Brown

Introduction

The philosophy of value tends to be concerned with factual judgments in relation to ethical choice, economic worth or adaptive decisions; that is, better and worse, the shoulds and should nots of moral conduct, the classification of things that are good or bad, or value as the outcome of instruction, deliberation and/or an intention to act. Since value can be attributed to subjective preference, feeling, habit and bias without rational justification, indeed, what we value most – family, friends – are of this sort, the account of value shifts from the nature of value itself to the objects of valuation, specifically to an evaluation of the legitimacy of the valuation; that is, the object of the value replaces the valuation of the object. Because they are subjective and weighted with self-interest, value-judgments are distinguished from truth-judgments or facts, though it can be argued that facts are the endpoints of valuations. Intrinsic or extrinsic value is conceived as an incentive or a lure to which a judgment is directed. An occasion of decision defines the value to which the decision pertains. The value is realized through its object or application. Value can apply to self-interest, as in avoiding pain and seeking pleasure, or to ethical acts that concern others and involve self-sacrifice. When value is an appraisal of outward worth, it becomes a judgment.

The universality of value in human cognition is such as to limit its application, generally to aesthetic and moral choice as in the value of a good act or a work of art. The object replaces the value, what it is and how it arises. Nor is there agreement on value in nature, whether value is intrinsic to the world or is projected outward by the mind. If value is unique to human mind and its interpretation is confined to art and ethics, the problem remains of its evolution or emergence, similar to that for consciousness. For most philosophers, value pertains to ethical choice. Dewey (1939) surveyed the range of its applications and conceded that value begins with impulse, though he focused discussion on evaluative judgments. These can be for what is good for the individual or what is good for others. The balance of the ego- and exo-centric, or the inhibition of self-interest for the good of others, is fundamental to moral

DOI: 10.4324/9781003535775-9

choice. Moral values would seem to be uniquely human, while the morality of nature is survival and reproduction, yet human valuations are imported from the animal ancestry.

For philosophers who think of value as a judgment, a rational comparison of good and bad, or better and worse, rather than a feeling, an inclination or a disposition, the same question arises. If value is moral judgment, say the value of truth or the good, where does it come from and how does it develop? When valuation is centered in an act of conscious judgment or in the object of a valuation, for example, the value of a good act, the process through which the valuation arises is diminished. As with other mental phenomena, antecedents become irrelevant once outcomes are clear.

This chapter is a speculation on value-creation and its continuity with other mental phenomena. The first question is, what is the origin of value in mind and world? Another approach is whether there is intrinsic value in objects or only in the mind of the observer. Are we drawn to objects of value or do we create value and impose it on them? Do objects have intrinsic value independent of mind? Is value transported to the world or imposed. Does it extend from mind into the concepts out of which objects are specified? In what form, if any, is value or its precursors in physical nature? If we begin with the physical world, do we find the antecedents of human value? If we begin with an evolutionary account of the mind, is it likely that value or its precursors can be found in primitive organism?

The earliest sign of value is interest or preference. To attend or to notice is to value one thing over another; indeed, one could claim that existence itself is the seed of valuation. Does a tropism become a bias, which becomes habitual, which becomes a preference, and finally a conscious desire? The selection of one thing or direction over another is a value. Value entails the consciousness of the implicit choice in preference. We do not value that for which we have no interest, nor do we have interest in things which, for us, are of no value. Interest is an early sign of valuation. This raises the question of how the value that grows out of interest is applied to external objects. Is value, along with feeling and meaning, transported outward through concepts into objects as worth?

If value is limited to conscious judgment, even if it arises in primitive life forms, the dependence on consciousness implies that, as with consciousness, value is either an evolutionary continuant or an emergent. Did value, or consciousness, emerge at a certain point in neural complexity, or does value – proto-value – appear in the lowest of organisms; if proto-value is ingredient in the earliest organisms it would appear at the onset of living systems. The question then arises, does value have its roots in tropisms, preferences and orientations, say in approach/avoidance, or in the attraction to pleasure and aversion to displeasure? If so, how do these inclinations lead to rational judgments? Presumably, value derived as interest or preference carves up the world into events, which in turn evokes beliefs that create facts.

Put differently, value selects events about which factual determinations can be made. This is the ground for consciousness of subjective aim and the intervention of reason. One can say that certainty in a fact is the endpoint of value-formation.

Value that arises in desire is the wish for a future object or desired course of action. To acquire a valuable object, to feel desire for something one wants, or someone who is loved, a person of incalculable value, is to wish to have or admire an object that is perceived as good or pleasurable. In such instances when the desired object is not present, valuation enters into a decision, whether emotive or rational, as to the best course of action to obtain the desired end. The valuation of the means to that end is, from the point of view of the quality of value, a trivial distinction. In cases where there is an immediacy of value in decision – the choice of the right path or response – preference is a pragmatic thread to adaptation. On this way of thinking, value is a direction to the better (more adaptive) of several possible actions.

This chapter takes an historical or diachronic approach to the evolution of value and the intra-psychic continuum from value as preference, say for pleasure, as in safety, warmth or food, or for what could be deemed good for the organism, to value as ingredient in desire. Conscious valuation is the outcome of a continuity of feeling that passes outward with objects. Indeed, value is perhaps the only mode of feeling that accompanies the object-development into the world. In the course of this process, the satisfactions of impulse individuate the attenuations of rational thought. The emotive quality of value impels action to what, from the standpoint of the agent, is the most adaptive or reasonable act. Values instilled in childhood are brakes on egocentric conduct, more like generic dispositions than reflective judgments, laying down unconscious habits through which character is effected in behavior. The evolutionary path from energy, as will, through feeling to the pursuit of the good is the self-realization of an act of cognition in a trajectory from raw impulse to conscious refinement.

Speculation on the Origins of Value

Value arises in desire as a mode of feeling. If desire is the wish for something, value is the justification for that wish. Value is the feeling that directs a desire to its object. The beginnings of feeling are surmised to have their onset as a progression from the physical to the animate as a transition from bi-directional energy in inorganic entities to directional feeling in living organisms. Specifically, isotropic energy is presumed to evolve to directional feeling, which is the life force that animates organisms. The continuum from energy to feeling and its subsequent evolution to drive are the basis for a pan-protopsychism in which living systems can be traced to the energic underpinnings of physical entities. Directional energy, as feeling, is the basis for growth. In each epoch of existence, feeling propels the entity through one full cycle of being.

How unity develops out of multiplicity, the reconciliation of (a sense of) inner wholeness and the perception of outer diversity, is an old problem in metaphysics. Does mind combine diversity to felt unity in the simultaneity of a mental state? The enfolding of disparate constituents binds them together. Temporality entails one-dimensional order in which feeling brings unification. Put differently, the manifold of an aggregate has unity as an event, that is, in process, not as a collection of discrete entities (Faber, 2004). To paraphrase Whitehead's well-known remark, the many become One (by entrainment in momentary process) and a new One is created:

> The many become one, and are increased by one. In their nature, entities are disjunctively 'many' in process of passage into conjunctive unity.
>
> (Whitehead, 1978, p. 21)

Or in Wordsworth:

> There is a dark
> Invisible workmanship that reconciles
> Discordant elements, and makes them move
> In one society.
>
> (Prelude: 355)

Act and Object: Feeling and Concept

The history of human mentality makes an important advance in the appearance of instinctual drive. The initial state entails a concentration of feeling and its distribution in the categorical primes that are its objects. The categories are pre-perceptual concepts that lead to objects; the feeling in drive (impulse, urge, will) refers to early stages in action that accompany drive categories. The feeling is inseparable from the drive category which partitions to sub-categories of implementation. For example, hunger as a basic drive category individuates to sub-categories of prey, stalking, capture, strategy, feeding and escape. The motility that implements the drive imparts the feeling, whether interest, fear, caution or the savagery of predation. Specifically, the drive *category* corresponds to early phases in perceptual development; *feeling* corresponds to early phases in action-development. Concepts are static frames innervated by feeling. The dynamic of feeling impels concepts to actualize. The combined *conceptual-feeling* transitions through image (thought) and emotion to actuality (see Figure 2.2.1).

Feeling is realized through action and, like action, remains partly in the mind. The body-image supports early segments in act-generation; even distal limb movement is only partly external. Action retains its locus in mind for the feeling of agent-causation. The feeling of will or drive at an early phase in the derivation of action provides affective intensity in concert with the drive category. *The combined concept and feeling is the source of emotion*, generally more intense at earlier (drive-close) phases, and progressively more restrained at distal (thought-close) phases. Actions mediate the feeling that is the dynamic of transition; perceptions mediate the categories or concepts that are its objects. The feeling-tone of developing actions, combined with the conceptual frame of developing objects, passes through segments of affective intensity to relatively affect-free acts and objects. That is, in human mind, pre-perceptions lay down self and image in a transition to the world; action imbues self and concepts with feeling to energize decision. Feeling is felt as a continuation into action of the implementation of ideas. The main contribution of action to mentality is not the idea or the action plan, which are products of thought and phases in the pre-object; rather, it is the feeling in will or drive, in desire and emotion, in agency, in the distinction of active and passive movement, in the intent and discharge of will in motility and the effectuation of thought as vocal or limb action.

The temporal lag in perception is equivalent to the readiness potential in action. Acts and objects are not outputs and inputs but develop in parallel through endogenous process. Acts are instigated prior to the consciousness of a decision to act, and objects are recognized prior to the conscious perception of what they are. The kernel of an incipient representation at the brainstem core, in conjunction with the diencephalic sources of instinctual behavior, propels action as drive-impulse into pre-perceptual categories. Feeling is the forward-going impulse enacted in bodily space. The lack of full detachment of actions from their subjective antecedents mitigates the outward flow of feeling. The effectuation of emotion in bodily action is display. Put differently, concepts lead to external objects; action leads to discharge in the world. But feeling remains intra-psychic; it appears in gesture because the action, which lays down the emotion, does not, unlike objects, fully detach from mind but is felt as belonging to the agent.

The relation of feeling to action goes back to the debate on *Innervationsgefühle* between Wundt and James. While awareness of active movement depends on recurrent collaterals of the action discharge, and is thus perceptual, the action-development contributes the feeling that flows into pre-perceptual categories. Specifically, feeling first deposits in drive categories as instinctual impulse; then, at subsequent phases, it is allocated to drive-derivatives and the concepts of desire. The distribution of feeling into concepts results in emotion, or the affective charge of personal concepts. The distribution of feeling in impersonal concepts, such as ideas, provides the intent or motivation for rational judgment. Reason does not grow out of emotion or the "moral sentiments" (Hume); it is infused and shaped by action-derived feeling as a directional factor. Perception and its preliminaries are static, fixed in the present (or the past realized in the present), while action is forward-looking. Action is clearly engaged when the vectors of drive are innervated, as in flight or fight (below), or when the intensity of emotion spills over from display to energetic action, as in escape, panic or rage. The relation of action to will is the direction of drive-impulse to satisfaction. Will is the impulse of drive carried into the agency of conscious volition.

Drive

Instinctual drive is the primary reservoir of feeling at the onset of action and the mental state. Feeling concentrates on potential at the inception of the state, initially as hunger (thirst). The urge or will to go forward is the core feeling in action; the categorical primes of drive are its core concepts. The drive has a conceptual aspect in the category to which it is directed, and an affective aspect in the feeling of directed action. On a recurrence model, such as microgenesis, in which mental states actualize and are replaced, hunger is the primordial self-preservative drive that sustains the organism to replicate itself and, later, to reproduce its likeness in progeny. Hunger is the primary allocation of feeling; it is the generative construct – impulse and category – that leads through thought and emotion to individuation and diversity. Food is the fuel of recurrence. The initial act of the newborn is to feed, by nursing or other means. The organism first has to survive. Survival is reinstatement. The hunger drive is in constant recurrence; this is the basis of self-replication. In the well-nourished where food is plentiful, the force of hunger is not felt but in the famished it takes precedence over sexual drive and other needs.

The sexual (reproductive) drive resolves out of hunger, retaining many of its properties; pursuit, aggression, submission and conflicts with rivals, as well as its appetitive and consummatory nature (Figure 3.1.1). The urgency of hunger gives way to the intermittency of reproduction. This accompanies a shift from the reinstatement of the individual to reproduction and generic replication. Hunger is essential for causal persistence of the organism, which is auto-replication, while reproduction of progeny is proxy replication. It may be incorrect to refer to the urge to reproduce in animals as a sexual drive; except in animals such as bonobos, it serves primarily for reproduction, not sexual pleasure. In humans, the drive and its evolutionary function have become separated, such that sexuality is dominant. An organism must survive to mate and provide parental care, but all things recur, with the novelty in each occasion a measure of the creativity of organism. One can say, the cycle of life distills to moments of experience continuously repeated.

Both hunger and reproductive behavior in animals are relatively stereotypical and organized about action, as feeling impels the organism to seek food and mating. In some organisms such as certain birds, the prelude to mating undergoes an extravagant expansion in displays, song and nest-building. Here, the drive is diverted from immediacy to the complex repertoires of reproductive drive. Such preparatory routines no doubt serve an adaptive function though, like the antlers of the extinct elk, far in excess of what should be necessary. In higher animals, the feeling that arises with action pours into primitive emotions; fear, pain and pleasure, and provides the momentum that carries the behavior outward. In humans, of course, under the influence of desire, which is a specification of drive, there is enormous diversity, say as hunger-borne desire leads to culinary habits and sexual desire refines the varieties of sexual pleasure.

Paul MacLean's (1990) four F's of drive – fight, flight, feeding and sexual behavior – resolve to two basic drives, hunger (thirst) and reproduction, and the two main vectors of approach and avoidance. The vectors of hunger are predation and defense, seizing prey and avoiding predators. These vectors, along with the hunger drive, fractionate to the sexual drive and its vectors of capture, escape and submission. The primary emotions associated with the basic drives are anger (aggression) and fear. The drives and their vectors are more or less programmatic in relation to categories of limited possibility. Thus, hunger impels a search for what is edible; sexual behavior is restricted, within species, to available and willing females and fortunate or dominant

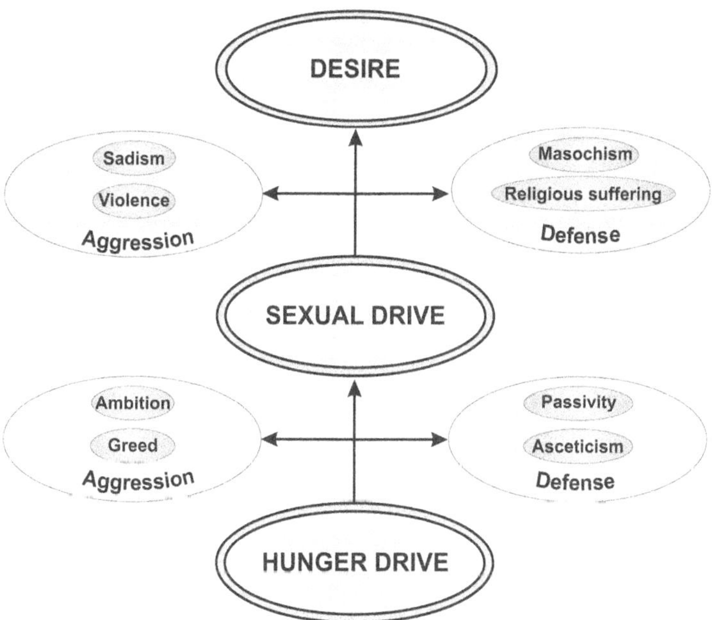

Figure 3.1.1 Hunger is directed to aggression and defense, or predation and escape. It individuates to sexual drive, then to desire, with ambition or greed in relation to the aggressive vector and timidity or retreat related to the defensive vector. Hunger partitions to sexual drive which is initially stereotypical, then partitions to desire and the varieties of interests and pleasures derived from the antecedent drives. Drive retains, in desire, the appetitive and consummatory features in the wish and its fulfillment.

males. The vectors can be conceived as a succession of approach/avoidance behaviors which trace down to paramecia (Schneirla, 1966).

The constellation of drive categories and the relation of primitive feeling to concepts – conceptual-feeling – lays down the emotions and is derived to desire and its objects. As derivatives, the emotions show traces of the antecedent drives, though usually mitigated in intensity and more individuated in quality. Thus, greed and ambition can be conceived as partitions of the aggressive vectors of hunger, while timidity and disgust are partitions of the defensive vectors. The sexual drive, which is emphatic when the pangs of hunger are too readily consummated – dinner as a precursor to sex – fractionates to pain avoidance and pleasure seeking, love and loss, affection and grief and the gradations of sadism and masochism. Fetish and perversion capture nicely the innervation of object-concepts by sexual feeling.

Emotion

Emotions are most often described as a response to external circumstance. A person is in despair over a loss or the absence of hope; frustrated because of an obstacle or the inability to achieve something; humiliated or proud on some occasion of importance; angry over a setback or disagreement. Affective states are also described in relation to other emotions, such as grief as a form of sadness, sorrow, anguish or as a form of depression, or ascribed to body physiology or chemical alteration in the brain. Fear is a prototypical response to a category of threat, apprehension is unrest about an impending event. Related affects – fright, panic, anxiety – are within the same category. Anger in a category of aggressiveness has rage at one extreme and irritation or annoyance at the other. Love is yet another category, with affection, devotion, passion and ecstasy referring to differing objects, conditions and intensities. Commonly, states overlap; jealousy and envy are distinguished by the need in jealousy for three individuals. The common feature is that emotions are internal states bound to concepts and described in relation to external events, similar states, conditions or categories. Accounts of emotion acknowledge the relation to concepts but for the most part they postulate a reaction to external conditions or an *association* of feeling and idea. The connection of concept and affect is by way of association (Lindsley, 1951) or libidinal cathexis (Freud), but not the fractionation of unitary conceptual-feeling into emotions and ideas.

The intensity of an emotion – how strongly it is felt – is related to the concentration of feeling; the quality of the emotion – what emotion it is – can be attributed to the concept. The perceptual event that elicits the emotion does so by arousing intermediate segments where conceptual phases in the pre-object, together with formative phases of feeling in the action-development, evoke an emotion that is related to the provoking event. On this interpretation, feeling does not combine with concepts – feeling and concept are aspects of a single configuration – but the concept, imported from perceptual experience, together with intermediate phases in action-formation, precipitates as emotion in an intra-psychic field at segments prior to exteriorization. An emotion points to revived and accentuated (neotenous) segments embedded in the final actuality, taking on its qualitative attributes from submerged layers in the inciting perceptual experience, and its quantitative intensity from earlier levels in action. The distinctness of the conceptual content to which the emotion is directed also obtains when feeling pervades an image, whether a memory image or one in the imagination, as in that aroused in expectation. The concept of an emotion is more likely induced by an external event, whereas that of desire tends to be related to a memory image (below).

Many taxonomies of the emotions have been assembled which itemize the emotions without a thought to their explanation. The claim here is that an inciting event, usually but not invariably external, is revived to evoke conceptual phases in the perception of that event, along with corresponding segments in action (feeling), to give specificity and intensity to the emotional state. Feeling in act-formation is the impulse of becoming; concepts in percept-formation prefigure the object that becomes. Put differently, the heightened subjectivity midway in the mental state –feeling derived from drive, concepts derived from instinctual categories – are complimentary aspects of a single configuration – an emotion – that rises into prominence when the dominant focus of the mental state is on earlier segments.

The transition from the necessity of drive, through the subjectivity of emotion to the final actuality encompasses the trajectory of a sequence of mental states, replicated each moment to evoke the imagery in each traversal. The intentional object of an emotion is not merely the external occurrence that appears to be its cause, since people respond differently to comparable events – the death of a close relation can incite joy, grief, relief and so on – but the idea to which the emotion refers and the experiential history that determines the impact of the inciting event.

In mild emotions, feeling is experienced by a self. The self has an emotion, just as the self has a thought. In strong emotions, there is less separation of self and feeling and emotion may consume the mental state. The individual is carried away by the emotion, and may say: "I was not myself, lost control or was overcome". The self feels anger, fear or love, but the emotion, when strong, points to an angry, fearful or loving self. In emotional states, the self is hostage to feeling, unable to generate competing thoughts. The implicit relation of self to emotion, and the felt relation of emotion to external events, have an intentional quality that depends on which relation is prominent in conscious experience.

Feeling fills conscious experience when it intensifies or generalizes. When feeling concentrates in one emotion, the concept recedes in the background. Intensity of feeling overwhelms the concept that determines what the feeling is about. In abstract or impersonal concepts, feeling is reduced. Emotion weakens when the concept dominates. Reason does not seek mastery of the emotions. There is no battle of intra-psychic faculties. Feeling wanes as concepts grow more abstract or complex, and conceptual prominence is diminished when feeling is intense. Feeling will intensify in abstract concepts such as liberty when the concept reduces to slogans that incite passion, and emotions subside when their conceptual frame widens or becomes more intricate. When a love for the one becomes a compassion for the many, the emotion, as Hegel noted, is more like an idea than a feeling; that is, the concept, when too inclusive, is more pronounced than the affect, which is diluted in the expansion.

Feeling is intrinsic to every concept, and every concept has an affective tone. Absent the concept, feeling has no object. Absent feeling, the concept lacks direction. The directedness of feeling in drive carries action to the aboutness of desire. Aboutness needs the momentum that feeling gives to ideas. It is the aim to definiteness. Feeling is the impetus for decision and its implementation in action. Action provides the direction of intentionality, concepts provide its object; that is, feeling gives the aboutness of the intentional, while the concept is what the intentional is about.

Desire

The object of emotion extracted from present experience is an idea, or a memory image that is experienced in the present. The satisfaction of the subjective aim, however, may be postponed indefinitely. Unlike other emotions that are encircled by their object (concept), desire tends to be for something pleasant, or the avoidance of the unpleasant; it points to the potential for subsequent feeling when the intention is realized or the object is possessed. Desire is the sublimation of will transmuted from instinctual impulse to conscious intent. The feeling in desire is twofold, partly to the pleasure of longing, in which the object is what is wished-for, and partly to the hope of its acquisition. The concept forecasts the object that desire is hoping for. Desire is a partition of drive that is diluted in consciousness to loosen its grasp on immediacy. Desire connotes a state of wanting. While an external object may or may not be present – one can wish to win the lottery or desire to have what one perceives – desire is present feeling, internal as a memory or thought image, the satisfaction of which is deferred to the future.

Value

Desire differs from other emotions in the priority of value. While the quality and force of emotions reflect the valuation given to the event – as noted, the same or comparable events evoke different emotions in different people – desire is more intimately related to personal valuation. As drive is the urgency of preference, desire is the mitigation of immediacy. Desire enfolds present feeling and the anticipation of future pleasure; value determines the desired object shared with the hoped-for outcome, which is felt as present in longing and in the desirability (worth) of what is longed-for.

There is a continuity in the twofold nature of desire – the wish and its satisfaction – each constrained by value. The need and consummation of unconscious drive becomes the wish for satisfaction of conscious desire. The implicit preference of drive becomes the valuation of desire. The fulfillment of drive is the worth of a desired object as subjective value becomes objective worth. One would not say of desire as of value that it flows into its object, for the feeling of desire is wanting what is absent or unobtainable. Desire looks to the future. Ordinary emotion does not usually have a quality of futurity; it is felt in the here and now.

Evolutionary constraints involve competition for survival and selection of the fittest. In drive, they specify the best available option. In perception, they involve sensory modeling. In other mental acts, there is selection by annulment, the carving of specificity by inhibition, and elimination of the irrelevant or redundant. There is a parallel between refutation as an explicit methodology and elimination as a tacit pattern. Selection is what remains after all else has been rescinded. The parsing of the many to the one is a general law of mind and nature. In life, value provides a constraint on desires that limits the possibility to realize them. There is a culling of desire by value, and a culling of value by character. In science, value is in the selection of topic, the isolation of problems and the choice of experiments designed to resolve them. The uncovering of fact entails the negation of error, similar to selection by elimination in other modes of cognition.

Value has an intra- and extra-personal complement, the latter the value of external objects. In desire there is a transition from mind to world in the conveyance of intrinsic value to extrinsic worth. On this interpretation, the distinction of intrinsic and extrinsic value is a transition from value as implicit, as habit or preference, to value as a conscious desire for something, to value as the worth that is attributed to the something that is desired. One says: "I want that because it is valuable" or, "Because it is valuable, I want it". This can lead to uncertainty as to which came first. "Did I love him because he was handsome", or "Did I think he was handsome because I loved him?" Value and worth straddle the mind/world divide. Value is not projected on barren objects but flows outward with the act- and object-formation. The lack of full detachment and the belongingness of action give value an external locus but keep it tethered to the mind. Concepts, however, objectify, leaving emotions behind as subjective phenomena.

Similarly, aesthetic values do not inhere in objects but are implicit in the first impression and subsequently "retrieved". That is, in the interpretation of an art work, tacit knowledge bypassed in the original perception is regained in successive revivals. The beauty or meaning in a work is the latent value that first orients the person to the work, and then recurs in conscious reflection.

Unlike emotions that objectify in display, the value of a desired object is a stream of feeling that begins in drive and flows into the actual or imagined object. The derivation of the drive repertoire to conscious desire and its varied manifestations is the main road of affect-development.

Value in the framework of ethics is intrinsic to the good, but the relation to the good, from a psychological standpoint, is arbitrary. A value-judgment is outside the agent as an external relation. Value assigned to good or positive ends or to outcomes of acts is not relevant to the nature of value itself. Someone can value greed, theft or hurtful pleasures. Ordinary values such as the *Golden Rule* or *love thy neighbor* are instilled as other-directed constraints on egocentric drive. The transposition of good and bad to right and wrong – the shift from intent to act – presumes that learned values, modified by experience, are drained of feeling to conform to reason. On this view, values consolidate as settled authority to replace the dynamic of process. Cultural and religious obligations provide added reinforcement. Emotion is not pruned from rational appraisal but returns, in the appraisal, as unconscious feeling.

Value determines the positive or negative valence of the objects that desire is seeking and channels desire to normative ends. It lays down the possibilities through which desire can be realized, the *do's*, *don'ts* and social norms by which the drives are shaped. Value is an injunction that carves the possible into the acceptable, constraining acts to conform to education, custom, duty, culture and experience, not as a judgment of good or bad, though it is recruited for this purpose, but as a resolution of the weight of competing interests. Desires express personality tainted by character, values are constituents of character with a trace of personality.

Conclusions

The co-temporal development of act and object gives emotion, with arousal of imagery on the pre-perceptual side and, on the action side, an intensity at phases prior to discharge. When feeling discharges into concepts as emotion, except for the primitive drive-based emotions such as panic or rage, its forward-going urge is attenuated. One could say that feeling surrenders impetus when it aligns with a concept. Act and object go on to completion but the activation of earlier segments of thought and feeling combines to give an emotion in which the quality of feeling – what emotion is – is related to perceptual imagery, and the quantity or intensity of feeling – how strongly it is felt – is related to phases in action discharge. The category or image gives the specificity of the emotion; the action-feeling gives direction and intensity to what is felt. The unity of act and object, or feeling and concept, is the process of becoming, which passes through intermediate segments in mind to actualize in the world.

The conceptual frame of the emotion – the category – enlarges at the expense of the feeling. Conversely, feeling intensifies at the expense of the concept. One can say the more abstract emerges from the more concrete. In the emergence from concrete to abstract, from the primal emotions to the subtlest and/or most general affect-ideas, intense feeling is drained from the concept and only the subtle, refined emotions remain. The relation of concept to feeling is a miniature of the relation of mind to brain, with concept a mental phenomenon and feeling related to physiology.

Desire retains the appetitive and the consummatory features of the drives from which it arises though with less urgency. Unlike drive, the self is conscious of desire and the desired object, a consciousness of the two stages, the wish and its satisfaction. Desire is the inheritance of drive, with vectors of pleasure seeking and avoidance of displeasure, the difference being the shift from immediacy to expectation, or need to wish, and the specification of the drive-vectors from a fixed repertoire to a multitude of possibilities. This transition is occasioned by the duration of the present and the arousal of content in the mental state. The direction taken by desire is determined by the value assigned to the desired object.

Value is intrinsic to desire; we desire what we value. Every act of conscious valuation entails an objectified wish. Value invests the objects that desire is seeking. The initial expression of value is existence, then attention distinguishes one event as important. Value begins with interest as one or more qualities are singled out for attention. To attend to one object at the expense of others – in animal or human mind – is the initial condition of value. Consciousness of interest is awareness of preference, while consciousness of preference takes a tropism to a valuation. At a basic level, value is an expression of preference, but how basic? Is a tropism a proto-value? The preference of frogs for certain insects, or insects for plants, or even the "preference" of plants for sunlight, may support an evolutionary origins of value but eliminates the subjectivity and consciousness essential to the intentionality of human valuation. In human mind, preferences "built in" to behavior such as handedness are not valuations, though when the agent is conscious of the preference it approximates a valuation.

3.2 Action-Feeling and Self-Conscious Mind

Jason W. Brown

Introduction

The Lord: How many Tathagatas have you honored, Mañjuśrī?
Mañjuśrī: *As many as there are the mental actions which have been stopped in an illusory man* (Mañjuśrī: Saptasatika: 213).

Philosophical speculation on action centers on conscious choice and interaction with the world, and has not, for the most part, taken into consideration the immediate ancestry of conscious phenomena and the patterns of dissolution which, in relation to isolates in the conscious stream, drop out once their outcomes are secured, while the symptoms of disruption, which are the basis for a reconstruction of the process, are perceived as anomalies in the normative state. As a result, two main components of voluntary action have been distinguished. One is that of agency and the implementation of an act such as grasping a cup or pulling the trigger of a gun. The other concerns the reasons and justifications for the action, such as the desire for a sip of coffee or wanting to use the gun to kill someone. The former is the feeling of willed action, the latter involves decision and self-object relations. The implementation of the action and its rationale are intra-personal though there is an extra-personal aim, while the effect of the action on objects is extra-personal. Action as bodily movement is conceived as physical output, mechanical and governed by the laws of nature; that of reasons, which relates to conscious choice, judgment and awareness of consequences, may or may not be causal or deterministic. To claim that the conceptual drivers of an action are physical effects of the brain and causally determined, whether or not it is correct, imports to mind the paradigm of empirical science and implies that causation is invariant in mind and world. It also raises the question if necessity is (or is not) incompatible with free will, or if agent-causation is essential to a free act. Philosophical studies tend to dismiss action as an irrelevant, to-be-clarified physiology, a causal output with little impact on the understanding of associated mental events. This chapter explores some of these questions in relation to a theory of the micro-temporal transitions that underlie the action.

DOI: 10.4324/9781003535775-10

Micro-Temporal Structure of Action

In that action and perception involve widely distributed regions in the brain, speculation on the succession of segments in the mental state, and specifically in the action-process, is possible only at a level of considerable generality. However, one problem for theory is the finding of billions of neurons in a pixel of neocortex, and perhaps a trillion connections; another is that structural components in an underlying *Bauplan* have, in the course of evolution, so individuated that their uniformity of organization is concealed in their complexity. A hierarchic organization over evolutionary layers leading through limbic and mesolimbic structures to neocortex and asymmetric action in the world entails a progression from bodily space and axial motility to neocortical motor areas for discrete innervation and distal limb action. The percept-development transports drive categories through concepts to objects. The act-development transports drive-impulse through feeling to acts. As we explained above (see *From Drive to Value*), concepts give the quality of emotion, and feeling gives the intensity of emotion.

The corresponding process in perception leads through a limbic transition of experiential memory to externalization and object space. The transitional series can incline to motility or perception depending on the dominance of feeling or concept. In both, process leads from a deep midline source in drive-based systems of brainstem, hypothalamus and/or diencephalon, through limbic formation to neocortex. The common transition through limbic segments accounts for the reciprocal influence of action-derived feelings and perception-derived concepts, the conceptual modulation of action and the affective and intentional bias in thought. Rather than a top-down transition, act and object begin at an archaic source and develop "upward" to final externalization.

The fundamental shift in the origin of drive is from the circularity of reflex to a synchronous act-object (Figure 2.2.3 of this volume). In reflex, a stimulus elicits a response that serves as a stimulus for another stimulus-response (S-R) reaction (Weizsaecker, 1939/1958). The argument here is that action and perception arise as multi-tiered representations out of the seriality of reflex. In this process, rhythmic systems of axial motility, such as human and animal gait, develop out of oscillatory systems such as the periodicity of circadian, biologic, respiratory and other cycles. A series of nested oscillators leads from earlier stages in evolution that support the gait and respiratory cycle to recent formations that underlie the "breath group", prosodic contour and the fine temporal pattern of digital and articulatory movement. Early music and dance are also realized through rhythmic phases. Evidence for the oscillatory foundations of action comes, *inter alia*, from the observation that purposeful finger movements appear at the crest of the rhythmic wave in resting tremor. Kinetic rhythms peel into bodily action (Bernstein, 1967). The pattern is one of a hierarchic series of rhythmic oscillators discharging at multiple levels.

In this derivation, objects develop through concepts out of drive categories; actions develop through feeling out of drive energy. Pre-terminal segments in perception are concepts or images; pre-terminal segments in action are feelings. The act-development transports drive-impulse through feeling to action. As we explained above (see *From Drive to Value*), the fusion of feeling with concept gives emotion. Concepts give the quality of emotion, feeling gives the intensity. Action provides the feeling that infuses concepts with emotion, as well as the intent to act and the forward momentum that brings aims and ideas to satisfaction. In this process, the dynamic of action (feeling) is the becoming of the epoch and the relative stasis of perception (concept) is the being, with their coincidence giving a becoming-into-being.

In sum, the co-temporal development of act and object gives conceptual-feeling, with arousal of concepts or images on the pre-perceptual side and, on the action side, an intensity of feeling at phases prior to discharge. As previously mentioned, act and object go on to completion but the activation of earlier segments of thought and feeling combine to give an emotion in which the quality or category of feeling – what emotion is – is related to perceptual imagery and the quantity or intensity of feeling – how strongly it is felt – is related to phases in action discharge. The category gives the specificity of the emotion; the action-feeling gives direction and intensity to what is felt.

Thus, with regard to intra-psychic process, the transition from potential to actual – the specification by elimination – gives the feeling of contingency and possibility behind every act. Action arises in drive and carries through to desire, which retains the binary quality of approach and avoidance. In desire, action specifies a feeling of intent directed to choices uncovered in the object-development. The arousal of phases prior to objectification gives ideas in the perceptual series and conscious feelings in the action series. The self is a precipitate of knowledge, drive and experience at the floor of the mental state, and is felt as an agent to the forward surge in action.

Agency and Choice

This account permits a new way of thinking on some fundamental problems in action theory. To begin, actions discharge in the body at a phase which, in perception, corresponds to pre-object concepts. An early phase in action is characterized by will or impulse; an intermediate phase by feeling and intent. The action is partly intra-psychic and, unlike an object which belongs to the world, is felt as belonging to the actor. The belongingness of action is part of agency, the feeling of willed activity and the intuition of a self that can instigate or cause an action to occur. The central phenomenon of conscious action is a self that can deliberately cause an action or mental image to occur. This can be a thought, a vocalization, a decision or an emotion. The action is purposeful; aims are felt as implemented by movements. Specifically, the feeling of agency stops with the action but its aim is for the outcome. It would be absurd, though not contradictory, to substitute an action such as combing one's hair instead of pulling the trigger if the aim is to shoot someone but the action would still be agentive, and even purposeful though intended for a different aim. Such displacements of action occur in apraxia, when they are still, it would appear, felt as purposeful.

With agency comes the problem of mental causation and the freedom of will. Agency is subordinate to volition, which implies freedom of thought or action. A voluntary act is willed and psychically unhindered. Volition is knowing an act is freely decided, while freedom is generally approached in terms of options, not open-ended possibilities. As agency is feeling and commitment, choice is experienced as open and not simply mechanical or causal. The freedom of choice is not resolved by chance, probability or randomness, which loosen the grip of causation but do not explain the feeling of willed activity. Similarly, a common assumption is that freedom of action, if it occurs, is infrequent and requires contingency and/or quantum indeterminacy, but this leaves self-initiation unexplained. A relaxation of constraints does not explain voluntary action but merely expands its range. Regardless of how one interprets a freely willed act, conscious intent is required. The problem of whether the self can cause an act to occur and whether, though caused, that event is freely caused, are separate problems. The self might underlie or precede an act that is felt to be freely decided even if, going back to arguments by Aristotle, the act is necessitated by circumstance, character and the experiential history of the individual.

We do not know how character and experience lead to action though this is the basis of volition and self-determination since any action, however unexpected, can be attributed to experience and would thus not be entirely free. On the other hand, the "ability to do otherwise" (see, *inter alia*, discussion in Pears (1963)) and O'Connor (1995) has, in my view, no explanatory weight, for it reduces to the psychology of choice and decision. Since every act materializes in the suppression of alternatives, for whatever act occurs there is always a "what if" for an act that does not occur. An outcome that is predictable even if the choice is not to act, or with awareness of the possibility to act otherwise, or if, in a gesture of freedom, a rational person should choose an irrational or self-destructive act, could still lead one to conclude that the act would be the only act that could occur given the sum of conditions at the point of decision. On the other hand, it is difficult to conceive of a voluntary action in the absence of all experience. Kant noted that a person free of attachments and without bias is someone without a history, without experience, loyalties, interests and without the knowledge to make an informed rational choice.

Another relevant feature is that choice usually boils down to two or three options. Most possibilities die still-borne. Once an option arises, it may fade and/or be replaced, or gain strength and sap the force of others. Options trace to the drives as preferences, which spill largely into opposing vectors, such as fight or flight. This might explain the usual binary nature of choice. Thought tends to settle on polarities, not gradations, for example, good and bad, mind and nature, universal and particular. These stabilities anchor transitions which are ignored, sublimated or imperceptible. There may also be a limit on attention to more than two or three ideas in the same or alternating states. Of course, not every choice is between polar opposites. Most decisions are this or that, better or worse, not right or wrong. Everyday choices would overwhelm an individual without preferences, or with apathy, indifference or weakness of will. Agency depends on predispositions to strip away a plenitude of possible actions leaving a few to surface to conscious choice.

A person unable to choose a meal from 50 entries on a menu, or a movie from a library of films, has a weakness in the capacity to decide, and with it an erosion of the feeling of agency, but not a loss if the individual can still peruse options and feel that choice is possible. Such a person resembles the memory prodigy described by Luria (1969) who was unable to select a thought from a flood of memories, much as in the short story of *Funes the Memorius* by Borges. Someone with too many options has a weakness of agency, though the freedom to choose remains. A person without options does not, for that occasion, have the ability to choose, and can be said to lack volition. This means that a person can have a sense of freedom to choose though unable to make a choice, or have a feeling of agency without the freedom to choose. A person is an agent even if forced to climb the steps to the gallows. An intra-personal impulse, not outer conditions, underlies the feeling of agency, but the purposefulness of agency must include the aim toward which the action is directed.

Volition

Decision-making can feel willed, but choice, though it accompanies intent, is not ingredient in agency, which is a feeling of willed activity in the production of images or bodily movements. The primary event is the action, not the contact of body and object. The feeling that mind acts directly on objects is telekinesis. The relation to the body is internal though the action has external consequences. Thus, in writing, it is the innervation of the hand that is holding the pen and the idea behind it, not the words on the page, though the pen feels like an extension of the hand as the words flow through it. There is a similar feeling in the baton of a conductor. In conversation the effect of one's words is not the basis of causal feeling but an extension of mental- to object-causation. The spoken or written word is a nexus of agentive feeling to the object (paper, reader, listener) on which it acts. One can speak of a writer causing the words on a page, or causing a reaction in a reader, but this chain of events has long left the writer. The endogenous feeling of agent-causation passes, deceptively, to the perception of object-causation. Indeed, it has been argued that the source of necessity in object-causation is the infant's reach for a (moving) target. Agency is a felt mental experience that begins with intent and ends in purposefulness.

Obstruction magnifies effort but not agentive feeling. A person feels an agent whether lifting a heavy weight or a needle. In cases when resistance is futile, as in a hanging, the impact is on volition not agency, since the will does not depend on external conditions. In Tolstoy's *War and Peace*, Peter, imprisoned, still feels an agent in thought, thus, he "cast his eyes upon the firmament, filled at that hour with myriad of stars. "All that is mine", he thought. "All that is mine is in me, is me. And that is what they think they have taken prisoner". What is lacking is not agency but the volition or freedom to do what one wants, and being conscious that, were the action to be permitted, the actor could carry it out.

Volition and agency are in conflict when the selection of one act voids the possibility of others; options are foreclosed even if new possibilities arise. The freedom to act without restrictions exists as a potential that embraces a multitude of possible acts, while commitment precludes all acts except that which occurs. More precisely, volition is the ability to select from a range of options; freedom is conceptual possibility; agency is the active feeling in the selection. Put differently, volition applies when an action is not coerced; agency applies when an action is (felt to be) instigated by the self; and freedom is self-determination and the expectation that a broad range of actions can be implemented. The concurrence of segments in act- and object-development aligns agency with becoming as feeling delivers the idea to motility.

Self and Decision

Drive arises from energic feeling as the initial manifestation of will and is refined over segments as conscious feeling and intent. Will is felt as a forward surge of the action-impulse arising out of instinct at the onset of the mental state, passing through the self as a coalescence of drive categories in relation to knowledge and experience. Instinctual drive lays down the self which precipitates out of experience and character. Action develops in concert with perception. The subjective in thought becomes the objective in perception. A subliminal action in every object corresponds to a tacit object in every act. Various writers have argued that thought develops in the delay before action, a delay that accompanies an expansion at segments within the forming act or object. The retreat to interioricity permits a consciousness of feeling as an impetus to thought and the ground of intent. We can act without thinking or think without acting but every mental state inclines to feeling or concept.

Through feeling, action is resolved to definiteness. The feeling in agency propels decision to finality, while reason is the adaptive quality of what is decided. Commonly, a focus on two or three alternatives accompanies a conscious assessment of the relative value of what is possible. In thinking, one or more ideas are rejected (vetoed), often implicitly, to arrive at the one that is chosen. Relating to Libet's (1985) work (see below), the idea of a conscious veto can be interpreted as a continuation into consciousness of the parsing – the selection-by-inhibition – that occurs at antecedent segments. Sub-surface proclivities are trimmed to uncover final specifications. Though acts are interpreted as the endpoints of a causal sequence, exposing an outcome is not the same as producing it. If decisions are uncovered, not selected, wherein lies the causal effect? The finding that action begins prior to consciousness of decision, along with studies of the readiness potential, are consistent with the unconscious origin of acts and objects and imply a duration that concurs with that implicated in the perceptual moment hypothesis (Stroud, 1956) and temporal lag.

Intent

As agency is the feeling of an active exertion of will, intent is the conscious desire to do something that anticipates or substitutes for an act. One might say that intention is knowing what one wants to do – the purposefulness of an act – while agency is the feeling of doing it. Intent is a weak feeling of agency, a desire to act in which a decision is made to do something that is not yet carried out. In one instance, there is an emphasis on the object of the action, in the other, on the preliminary feeling. Agency is the conscious implementation of intent, as intent is a tributary of will. Intentions do not inevitably lead to actions but they do imply preferences or decisions. Perhaps one could say that intent is to decision as will is to action. Intention can accompany agency, as when I intend to say or do something but fail in the attempt, say, finding the right word, or when I "change my mind", yet there is a feeling of agency in the effort. Agency may pass through intention as it spills into an act. However, unlike agency, which is restricted to bodily or mental activity, an intention, say to lift a book, entails the knowledge I can lift it. I do not intend to do the impossible. Intention requires knowing what I want to do even without the capacity to do it. I intend to (try to) win the race though I may not be fast enough, but I would not intend to have a race with a horse. Knowledge participates in decision, with intention a combination of knowledge and desire (Anscombe, 1963). Perhaps intention is less the knowledge that inspires an action than the feeling of knowing what to do, with desire an accompaniment, a rationale or justification for the decision.

The desire to lift a book has a trace of the directionality and self-initiation that are more strongly felt in agency when the book is actually lifted. We see the forward direction as an inclination to act. The futurity of intention distinguishes it from agency and emotion which entail present feeling. Agency is a more bodily feeling than intention. The closer to the world surface, the less the feeling is grounded in the body. Intention entails a conscious if implicit choice that can resolve indecision even if its aim is ill-defined. It may even be that intention arises in the making of a decision rather than being a forecast of its selection or implementation. One can think of intention as a specification of desire that expresses a wish or objective biased to action more than to objects and directed to future satisfaction. A thing desired is valued and the impulse to act is an expression of a desire. Perhaps we could say that desire is feeling directed to things (events, etc.) of value, and agency is feeling directed to acts that achieve desired or valued ends. The distinction concerns the distribution of feeling into concepts or actions.

Freedom and Agency

Free will is a conflation of volition and agency, making an appearance when freedom of action is appended to the exercise of agency. One might say that freedom is for the many, action for the one, with free will combining adventure in the world with the mind's imaginative reach. Freedom is a catalog of potential; agency is a dynamic of forward-directed activity, a manifestation of will in relation to action as drive energy flows into movement or mental content. In sum, *agency is inner activity in relation to purposefulness; volition is the menu of possible actions, and free will is their unholy alliance*. Ultimately, freedom must be tested to be more than theoretical, and action must be rational to merit the freedom that volition requires. To paraphrase the poet, lack of freedom is more than "vague longings bred by want of power"; freedom is the capacity to act in accordance with rational desire.

One aspect of free will is the ability to do otherwise; another is the ability to freely decide. With respect to the former, even if decision is conditioned at unconscious phases, given the postulate of a conscious veto, there is a potential to arrest the action if not do otherwise. If the choice is a film or concert, or something better or worse, the individual is always free to do nothing. In fact, the necessity of choice can itself be an obstacle to freedom. Inaction is no less a decision than action; to not make a choice is also a choice. In an occasion of decision, choices are like competing tendencies within or between categories with the potential for further elaboration. Preference becomes priority as recurrent traversals establish a relative dominance of one path over another. Feeling as intent "nudges" an idea to finality.

If we set aside agency as inner feeling, and concentrate on the freedom of choice, we can ask whether decision is effected in consciousness or imported to consciousness by submerged predispositions and, if the latter, what accounts for the belief that thoughts, plans and actions are freely chosen? What role in the origination and implementation of ideas is played by consciousness? If options are derived from presuppositions, inherent bias and the growth of preference over an iterated series of mental states, deliberation is a sideshow, yet still we believe that informed conscious intent is central to decision. Further, for an actor to state the reasons for an action when those reasons are the analytic endpoints of the pre-suppositional biases that underlie them is to accept surface justifications as inciting sources.

In simple actions such as purposeful finger movement, studies show that the onset of action is prior to conscious decision. The decision is primarily when to move the finger, not whether to move a finger or make a fist, since the choice is fully constrained by the experimental conditions. The subject can, and implicitly does, decline to move the finger until it actually moves. Could one say that since the action is pre-decided, the duration up to movement is that from generalized activation to specific intent? Further multiple mental states would be required for a single act or object. It also has to be noted that, finger movement is not that simple, but likely develops out of axial and postural motor systems through the proximal to the distal musculature, which requires some duration. The quota of feeling that accounts for intent is what is felt to impel the act. Other studies of unconscious cognition (masking, priming, etc,) show unconscious activation. These studies provide a strong challenge to the claim that volition arises in consciousness, and they are consistent with a before/after traversal from the archaic (unconscious) to the recent (conscious) in brain structure.

With deliberation, choice is less likely to be fully specified before it becomes conscious. The act must traverse segments in which the quality of feeling and the persuasiveness of ideas, regardless of their unconscious attribution, are options unique to the individual. While an informed rational person usually makes informed rational choices (are we to say unconscious decision is rational?), freedom is not necessarily in selecting the most rational choice but in the license to be who you are to make it. This includes the emotion that carries value to commitment. The individual is not a calculator that computes an objective outcome, but a person who brings a history to every decision. Decisions that are not the most rational may be a sign of ignorance, egoism or impulse, but they are also expressions of personhood, namely, the freedom to decide in conformity with one's feelings and character. Freedom owes to the dispositions of the agent, asserting the freedom to act according to personal desire, interest, bias and experience.

Feeling, not thought, is what drives and consolidates choice. What sways decision are feelings applicable to that individual. Given the primacy of feeling in organism, the will or the impulse to action is, as many philosophers have maintained, of all mental phenomena the most likely to be a direct experience of reality or the least likely to be illusory. A will is not free of ancestral claims, but the sense of free will or unhindered choice, leaving aside what constitutes a limitation on freedom, is too powerful to be dismissed without an account of how the phenomenon comes about. I would argue that the self, and act or object, occur as ingredients of the same epoch.

In the mental state, the self is antecedent to act and idea, a predecessor, not necessarily a cause. The relation of self to object or image gives a private theater that is the basis for consciousness. The epochal nature of the state entails simultaneity of phases until the state actualizes, at which point the agent becomes conscious of the succession, or the relation of self to image gives consciousness. This depiction of the mental state does not preclude the possibility of causation, especially in the replacement of one state by another, since the replacing state overlaps earlier phases in the preceding one. A causal effect across epochs would reinforce and supplement the base of the state prior to its actualization.

With regard to free decision, given a choice between two conscious options, does agency occur when the individual makes the final choice or when the option not selected fades away? Does the person feel an agent to an act unaware that alternatives have been eliminated? A final choice occurs when options are disempowered by the surviving course of action, which occurs implicitly even if the person feels that a displaced option has been intentionally rejected. The feeling of agency arises in the implementation of an intended event as well as in the final selection when other options have been discarded.

The question of causal necessity arises in relation to agency. If one conceives an action as the outcome of a transition that begins with instinctual drive, not as a circulation in consciousness of competing reasons or an externalism that ignores the action structure, the momentary pre-history of an action is critical. Early phases associated with (animal) drive that give rise to instinct-driven acts cannot be said to be freely decided, while acts with a dominant focus on phases that correspond to emotion, and consequent limitation of choice, may not have the rationality to justify being described as free. This label then applies largely to conscious acts that require a reasoned decision.

In a choice between competing options, if one option is reinforced over recurrent states such that its competitor is gradually replaced, how are we to describe the selection process? The dominant content arising from unconscious experience has a conceptual and emotive bias. The accrual of dominance over repeated volleys can be described as causal but is this true of the final choice if there is no actual selection but a dropping out of alternatives? The self is ingredient in decision but cannot be said to cause it. The actual cause is the resolution of one line of thought or intent by a reinforcement of the axis of its growth.

Conclusions

On this account, the self "stands behind" a decision but most likely does not cause it to occur, yet the final decision is not indeterminate since it is conditioned by past and present experience. Agent-causation is an uncovering of the selection and the feeling of its causal effectuation. Unlike the passage of drive into action, which in animals is more or less direct, choice is a realization of the potential for multiple outcomes. Individual freedom can be construed as the self-actualization of one's own character including personal experience, knowledge and emotion, along with the ability to act without extra-corporeal constraints. It is useless to ask if an act would be the same at another time if conditions were identical since there is novelty in events and in growth of personality. Novelty makes room for freedom but is not itself the freedom we are looking for. Self-expression will differ according to the individual life-experience out of which the self consolidates, but the individual must take responsibility for who he or she is, as others in moral judgment have a responsibility to consider formative history and circumstance.

3.3 Thought and Belief

Jason W. Brown

Introduction

One of the more intractable problems in psychology is the nature of thought, not least because of its privacy, fluidity and elusiveness, the uncertainty of how thought comes in contact with the external at one end and the self at the other, and the tendency to fracture thinking into various modalities – reason, belief, reflection, introspection – each of which is a topic for a separate analysis. It is well enough to say with the *cogito*, I think, but quite another to say what thinking is or how it occurs. Not only does thought span a range from the rational to the delusional, the unconscious to conscious, from the spontaneous to the effortful, the emotional to the abstract, the creative to the habitual and modes such as musical, mathematical, chess and, I would add, memory and perception, but the diachronic relation to experience and knowledge.

One essential feature is the relation of subjectivity to the world, a relation that is central to that of belief and fact. Another feature is that thinking can be ambient or focal with subliminal phases often in the background, punctuated by an occasional focus of conscious attention. Thinking is in relation to a thinker, a self that can feel causal to the act and content of thought. Further, there is the problem of how thought or conceptuality arises, recurs, has an aim and direction and leads to action.

My intent is to survey the relations between perception, memory, belief and thought, without diving into long-standing philosophical arguments or cognitive studies of "components" in memory, "assembly" models in perception, language of thought, or different applications, such as inference, implication and so on. The aim is an overview of the common basis of these activities which, I would claim, all evolve out of drive and drive-category, or action and perception, in animal behavior. The approach requires the setting-aside of standard views for a re-thinking of perception as an active, out-going process, an approach that can help resolve the pervasive tensions between conflicting interpretations of the self/world divide.

DOI: 10.4324/9781003535775-11

Perception

The key to a theory of mind is, and has always been, the nature of perception. According to the prevailing model, (visual) perception is passive, receptive and unmediated, with mental phenomena conceived as secondary to the input and assembly of non-conceptual sensory data. There is progressive construction of objects with projection outward to the world and inward to experience and recognition, with thought occurring as a post-perceptual capacity. There is no awareness of the sensory data that are presumed to be ingredient in the process, with the wholeness of perception assumed to result from the connectivity. This theory has conditioned an account of mental "faculties" as interactive agencies, and the result, I would claim, has been a fatal impasse in our understanding of mind and brain. Alternatively, perceptions are the endpoint of a micro-temporal development that begins and remains intra-psychic (chapter on *Time and the Dream*). Thought and memory arise within this process as elaborations of pre-object conceptual phases. In effect, thought amplifies the conceptuality concentrated in the object. Put otherwise, thought develops at proximal phases in the object, while objects (objectified images) actualize at a distal phase.

Memory aims at reproduction, and approximates thought to the degree it is incomplete or unsuccessful. The experiential world of perception that memory seeks to reproduce is the aim of rational thought which attempts to describe some features of reality that are relatively unnoticed. One can say that perception mirrors reality; memory reproduces it and thought describes it. In expanding the fixed world of reproduction, thought creates a deeper, even an alternate vision of the real. Perception discloses what is actual (present), memory what has been (past), and thought what might be (future) or a deeper understanding of the real. The diffusion and malleability of memory is the basis for the inexhaustibility of thought. The less complete an act of thought, the closer to tacit knowledge and the greater its remainder.

How far concepts reach into outer experience is a problem for direct perception or passive receptivity, but dissolves on the view that perception is an active process and that experience is a final phase (discussion in McDowell, 1994). Recognition is not post-perceptual; it is a conceptual phase embedded in perception. Even the failure to recognize an object – say a Rorschach picture – is evidence of a conceptual transition in the lack of match to a familiar concept, as well as the effort to frame a concept within which the picture has a place. Thus, we think up the facts and recognize objects before they are consciously perceived. Facts are the endpoints of thinking, outcomes, not inputs. Objects are the endpoints of perceiving, derivations not constructions.

Belief

Belief is a mode of thought that is directed outward in which the relation of mind to world is prominent. The relation of thought to externality is analogous to the relation of belief to fact, and for both belief and thought we can ask, do they arise on the facts that support them, or do they generate, or at least delimit, the facts on which they appear to depend? The same question – which comes first, mind or world? – can be applied to all mental phenomena. However, with belief there is a pressure to certainty and a relation to the truth-status of facts. In ordinary language, beliefs may be true, false or uncertain, while facts are presumed to be true, or provisionally so. There is a transition from experience and knowledge to thought, and to belief as thought takes on direction. We can say, preliminarily, that thought is *implicit* belief when it is directed to objects (facts), and it is *explicit* belief when this directedness is conscious and intentional. The coincidence of conscious belief and impersonal fact is truth.

Ordinarily, belief and knowledge are defined in terms of truth, with knowledge applied to true belief, and belief applied to irrefragable knowledge. This definition requires that belief and knowledge – the *I believe that*, and the *I know that* – must be in relation to true fact to be analogous when knowledge and belief can both be erroneous – one can have a false belief in spite of factual knowledge, such as common superstitions in educated persons (astrology), and fallacious knowledge can often, even serendipitously, provide the underpinnings of true belief. One can have vast knowledge together with unjustified belief (racism). One can presume to know things that are false (political opinions) and one can believe things that are fallacious or without evidence (alien visits to earth). There are visual illusions of which we are conscious (duck/rabbit; Necker cube) and others of which we are not (constancy effects), as well as in pathology (micropsia; inversion of objects). Perceptions may be unreal with or without a belief in their reality, and individuals can be uncertain whether they are the authors of their own thoughts and memories. We learn from such cases that certainty is not inextricably bound to the content to which it applies, that conviction in belief is often more powerful when evidence is wanting, and that the facts on which rational or scientific certainty depends can as readily be misconstrued as the beliefs to which they conform.

For philosophy, knowledge is justified true belief, but much of our knowledge is unconscious and many of our beliefs are unjustified. We can say to the same sentence (e.g. that camel urine is medicinal), I believe it is true but I don't know it for sure, or I know or have been told it is true but I don't believe it, so understanding the relation of fact to belief, of belief to experience and how beliefs take on conviction, is of importance to a theory of knowledge, while knowledge is the sum of available and potential beliefs or memories, or what is known and generally accepted to be true. Most of our knowledge is inaccessible, though demonstrated in action, whether the collection of acts and decisions over a lifetime or such procedures as riding a bicycle or knotting a necktie. Early experience that goes into character is irretrievable. What is recollected may be in a more superficial relation to the personality than what is forgotten (not repressed in the Freudian sense), while the inaccessible is often of greater influence on behavior than what is remembered.

From an externalist standpoint, facts may be self-evident (it is raining) or they can be based on evidence that accumulates to justify the belief (Mike Tyson was a great boxer), or arise from a hypothesis that requires proof (the curvature of space). Some facts arise through reason and many from authority, but most facts are perceptions to which beliefs conform. From an intra-psychic standpoint, beliefs emerge as modes of thought, which in turn are shaped by the facts to which they correspond. The foundational belief is that of an opposition between subject and object – inner and outer – and that self and world exist and are real.

Nietzsche wrote, consistent with the priority of the Will, "the greater part of conscious thinking must be counted among the instinctive functions". In animals, approach and avoidance are instinctual reactions deep in evolutionary history, almost reflexes and distinct from belief in ways other than complexity. Beliefs are specified out of the knowledge base to arrive at fact by intuition, reasoning or observation. Ancestral dispositions derived from drive-categories give rise to concepts delimited by experiential knowledge and adapted to the world. Given the instinctual origins of a mental state, it is likely that concepts fractionate out of categorical primes.

The aim of perception is a veridical object. The aim of belief is coherence with fact. The aim of thought is satisfaction in a rational outcome aroused out of a context that subsumes other facts as data for its justification. Thought involves a suspension of the definiteness that is the aim of belief. When thought resolves to an unhindered focus with a feeling of certainty and when finalities are constrained by reality, thought shifts to belief, the truth of which is reinforced by evidence. Thinking becomes belief when it reaches a certain endpoint. The primary stream of belief-formation is the carving of thought to fact. The transition from (a set of) ideas to specific beliefs is, ideally, from the plausible to the irrefutable. The aim is to truth or reality but an ambiguous generality is often preferable to a too hasty precision.

Belief and fact differ in that fact, by definition, *is true* and *it is true* whether or not it is perceived or believed, while a belief can be a false interpretation or distortion of fact or it can ignore fact entirely. Belief is intra-psychic; fact is generally relegated to the world. In ordinary discourse, to know something is to believe it. I know this is my right hand (Moore), and I believe it to be the case, though disorders of body image and the confusion of right and left question the veracity of common sense belief. However, it is more natural to say, *I know this is my hand*, not that *I believe it is*. This is because knowledge is the ground of belief, and common sense beliefs, which are part of the "structure" of knowledge, are accepted implicitly. Belief is derived from knowledge to prefigure perceptual fact. This does not mean that a belief is formed before the facts are known but that a phase of thought within the perception precedes its factual outcome.

Fact has been defined as true belief, but the belief does not make the fact true. Dream, myth and fantasy are not true facts even if one believes in their personal, symbolic or metaphoric significance. Facts are uncovered truths, and the uncovering is what turns an object into a fact. Once fact is established, the belief that gives rise to objects is exchanged for the objects that arise from belief. In this exchange, the concepts that give rise to facts that become implicit once the truth is decided. Propositions fill the space between beliefs and facts. If a fact is in the world and a belief is in the mind, a proposition is at the boundary. The proposition is a mental or realized statement that partially leaves the mind like other actions, though retaining a thread to the agent. Propositions are one of the means by which beliefs externalize.

Certainty and Conviction

Categories at the inception of belief support the feeling that leads to conviction even without the facts to support it. Conviction is feeling derived from will in the satisfaction of need, which can usurp the role of evidence. Certainty is the satisfaction of a conscious resolution of value. Certainty applies to the rational content of an irrefutable belief, while conviction refers to the intensity of feeling that the belief enjoys. Although the boundaries are imprecise and the terms are often used as synonyms, certainty is more appropriate for the impersonal while the personal is more likely to inspire conviction. Moreover, one can have factual certainty for an uncertain belief (red wine is healthy) or certainty without conviction, as when a belief is of little personal concern, while conviction occurs for personal beliefs (religious, delusional, mythological) for which certain knowledge is lacking. Certainty is a more rational conclusion; conviction is more like a feeling, though some writers, notably Wittgenstein, have conflated them to feeling. There is also the sense that conviction is more likely to lead to action. Perhaps one could also say that certainty, because it is closer to the perceptual surface, is open to a change in evidence, while conviction, because it is propelled by need, is more resistant.

In sum, categories of core drive (with instinctual response subdued) lay down dispositions in relation to the knowledge base, including experiential and impersonal memory. The awakening of knowledge in the perceptual component of the mental state rouses implicit or common sense belief, which serves as a guide for everyday behavior. On becoming conscious, implicit knowledge shifts to ideas or proto-beliefs, in which conviction can be established and truth can be determined. Thought generalizes and clarifies over successive mental states by way of recurrent volleys and/or the importation of accessory data. Early segments in the individuation of object-concepts are rapidly traversed in the absence of self-consciousness, but can diverge from the main path of perception to nascent feelings and novel ideas. Ideas (concepts) emerge as forerunners of perceptual fact. Conscious belief, knowing that one knows, arises between the final fact and the mediating idea, with certainty the outcome of a winnowing of potential to an objectified image. Concurrently, in the passage of action from instinctual drive to conscious effectuation, feeling aligns with ideas (concepts) to deposit impulse and emotion. The degree to which the concept (belief) approximates the final object (fact) determines whether there is certainty or conviction. Certainty applies to established fact, while conviction depends on intensity of feeling.

Delusion

The psychology of belief is enriched by a study of an irrational false belief with conviction, as is prominent in the extreme of delusion. Efforts to understand delusion have been devoted largely to descriptions of the different forms of delusional thought, ranging from the paranoia of psychotics to the grandiosity of tertiary syphilitics. Much emphasis has been placed on psychoanalytic interpretations and the penetration of thought by feeling (review in Bortolotti, 2022) without a general theory of the nature and origin of delusion and its relation to ordinary thought. Delusions may take on features that relate to the individual personality or circumstance, which may account for their specificity. There are cases in which a confabulatory delusion, such as someone who insists he won a million in the lottery, seems plausible. The Cotard syndrome (the belief one is dead) may owe to anhedonia and life-fatigue. In the Capras syndrome, a spouse or close relative is taken as an imposter though other individuals are correctly recognized and there may be a comparable reduplication of the home. Perhaps the delusion can be explained in part by the greater affective significance of the "imposter". I described a couple with a *Capgras a deux,* an elderly demented woman who thought her husband was a young man trying to seduce her, while the husband, with a small left temporal stroke, subsequently developed the complimentary belief. A similar interpretation might apply to the Clerambault syndrome, the delusion that one is loved by another person. The imaginary lover – often a doctor or celebrity – has a specificity and recurrence that point to a personal need. With regard to paranoia, I have speculated that it represents the emergence in wakefulness of the dream self, a passive victim to its own imagery. The interests and experience of the person could explain the paranoid content.

Most beliefs are formed early in life as experience enlarges. Early unconscious beliefs, often referred to as folk beliefs, are to some extent a part of the animal inheritance, but are largely acquired in childhood The infant's belief that a parent is protective, that a pet dog is friendly, that some foods are tastier than others, that stairs and hot stoves are dangerous, derives from experience with such objects or occasions. As perceptual experience accumulates, implicit beliefs form a foundation for later thought and imagination. From beliefs acquired in perception, there is a continuity to communal (societal, tribal) beliefs, those shared with others and accepted by authority, and to beliefs that are personal and individual, such as self-importance or hypochondria. When thought becomes as real as perception, belief in the impossible or improbable occurs, such as speaking to God, alien visitations and the like.

The greater the implausibility, the stronger the conviction and the weaker the factual basis.

In the transition to delusion, the imaginative idea or false belief tends to become encapsulated and isolated from other beliefs. The idea objectifies and has the vivid reality of perceptual fact. Generally, the susceptibility to delusion depends on an altered mental state. It would be unusual to see a fully normal individual having a fixed delusion, though strong opinion can take on delusional features. The boundary between a false belief that is tolerable, such as a religious belief, and one that is pathological, is determined by its individuality, contextual inconsistency and the conviction for the belief content.

Irrefutable belief may depend on true fact, in which case we can say that the belief is certain. When the belief is false but still maintained in spite of efforts to persuade the individual of the truth, we speak of conviction and irrationality. Conviction is closer to need and can be independent of evidence, while certainty tends to be less intense, and is closer to fact or proof. In religious belief as in delusion, conviction develops out of drive-based feeling in relation to need and will. A belief is an idea directed to an object or state of affairs. The idea may be justified or not; it may be more or less certain, it may become a focus of attention, may persist, recur or vanish, but it does not, in itself, gain or lose intensity. Conviction is the feeling of absolute certainty in the truth of a belief, whether or not the belief is true, while the strength of a belief is the strength of conviction in the belief, not of the belief itself. In pathological cases, it is not that the belief grows stronger, but that conviction in the belief intensifies.

Delusion and conviction arise together. In schizophrenia, the rustling of leaves becomes a whisper, which gradually takes on hallucinatory and/or paranoid content. The sense of reality for hallucination does not usually occur immediately, but requires a recurrence of the image or support by other modalities; e.g. an hallucination of a face is recognized as an image until it begins to speak, at which time it is perceived as real (see *Time and the Dream*). The appeal to another modality is not dissimilar from delusion, where the idea is not falsified because of a disregard for facts that would lead to disconfirmation. Feeling accrues as the belief develops. It is likely that, for the subject, the process that makes hallucination real is the same process that makes delusion feel true. The veridical requires a negation of falsity. We accept more than we doubt, the so-called confirmation bias.

Thoughts objectify as beliefs in dream and psychosis or in the reality of imagination in those who are impressionable. It may be that delusions are fragments in proximity to dream, along with the more intense feeling of early cognition, such that the idea (delusion) and the feeling (conviction) are carried into conscious thought as an autonomous construct that, like the conviction of the truth of dream and the reality of the dream image, is resistant to the logic of an otherwise normal mentality. This would give the delusion its wish-like quality, while the feeling of conviction would result from the closed universe of the content and its derivation out of drive-energy. On this way of thinking, the delusion arises as a nucleus of primitive mentation. In pathology it may replace a gap in memory. For example, I treated an elderly lady who fell and hit her head and was amnesic for the episode, but as she gradually recovered, she had the delusion that men were in her bedroom attempting to rape her. This was interpreted by staff as a possible deterioration but the delusion faded as she regained full recall. We learn from delusion that, in the natural course of things, belief-formation is prior to fact.

What is puzzling in delusion is the lack of interest in or even denial of contradictory evidence in spite of, to others, it's obvious falsity. The delusion may go against the person's experiential knowledge, which may contribute to its content but not to its refutation. Perhaps there is a relation to denial, though this refers to the presumed suppression of painful ideas, not evidence as to their reality. In this sense, the delusion is an island in cognition resistant to factual knowledge.

In sum, we learn from delusion that the relation of belief to fact can be tenuous, that some beliefs may be resistant to fact and that fact may not inspire a complementary belief. The wish-like quality of delusion, and much of ordinary false belief and superstition are accepted as real or true in the denial of facts that should figure in their refutation. In dream, the conviction of the reality of thought or image occurs in the lack of comparison to an alternative. And as in dream, false beliefs and delusions, along with the conviction of their truth, are a fortress that is impregnable to the very experience on which belief depends. If false beliefs satisfy instinctual need – a desire, a fear – conviction would also be the manifestation of instinctual will directed to a drive-derivative.

Knowledge

Apart from irrational conviction, belief seems more tenuous or malleable than knowledge, though both are part of, and cohere within, a common matrix. We can add to our knowledge, say when we first learn that Abuja is the capital of Nigeria, but without justification can we say we are certain this is so? Perhaps the capital has changed or the source was mistaken. To believe implies the possibility of error. Belief is more fallible than knowledge. We could say that belief becomes knowledge when it is shown or accepted to be true. Knowledge consists of an enormity of fact, much of it inaccessible, while belief is dedicated to states of affairs that are not invariably factual. Once such states are accepted as true, they sink into the pit of knowledge.

Language evolves as a branch of perception and action, in relation to those (frontal, temporal) areas implicated in these functions. Though we speak of our knowledge of syntax or vocabulary, we do not speak of a belief in a grammar or the truth of a syntactic form, though the ability to communicate through language owes to its adaptation to perceptual fact. Knowledge of a grammar is commonly described as competence, in which a speaker can be said to access an unconscious system of grammatical "rules", conventions or regularities though often unable to specify what procedures are being employed. It is argued that syntax generates novel utterances from such rules. Are the rules part of the knowledge base? Does this include their implementations as well? How is the facticity of knowledge resolved with the novelty of production? Apart from proper use, what would it mean to say that knowledge of a language is true fact?

Knowledge in language entails the ability, through the mediation of thought, to actualize meaningful utterances. Thought is so closely bound up with language that individuals may discover what they are thinking by what they say or write. Are domains of knowledge and components of performance segregated *ab origo*, or is the entire knowledge base activated for each separate thought or conceptual frame with improvisation and individuation to relatively autonomous systems? In pathological cases, when access to knowledge is severely limited, speech is reduced with minimal productivity, wit or conversational fluency.

Knowledge is often viewed as a storehouse of inter-connected facts, with the mind conceived as a blank slate that is filled in by experience, while everyday beliefs are assumed to grow into facts out of instinctual dispositions. The fractionation to speech by way of thought conforms in this respect to the directionality of belief. That is, the specification of a thought to a proposition is analogous to the realization of a belief in a fact. An immensity of dormant knowledge awakens and partitions as the occasion requires. How are unconscious systems targeted and separately activated? What determines how thought and belief arise from their unconscious origins. Moreover, thinking requires suppression of possibilities other than those which are realized or contemplated. Inhibition of irrelevance is as important as activation of salience. Since a memory or perception can, as for Proust, open the floodgates of what has been forgotten, it seems likely that the whole of one's knowledge must be available at the onset of each mental state, and then massively constrained for the relevant domains to be sorted out and derived into thought or action.

The problem is deep, perhaps insoluble, but it is likely that thought develops on an antecedent background of instinctual categories along with the learning that goes on within them (predation, mating, maternal care). The "structure" of knowledge – what actualizes and what is available – is infinitely complex, nested and inter-related, a union of drive and category, feeling and concept, that, in relation to language, individuates through the knowledge base to a variety of conscious phenomena (belief, reason, imagination and so on). This process goes through a succession of overlapping sub-categories (language, culture, musical and mathematical ideas, technical proficiency, historical facts, literary works etc.) out of which specific items resolve. Over time certain of these differentia can become more or less automatic or habitual, while others enlarge to novel worlds. The potential for cross-activation is essentially infinite since any item can relate to any other item within and across categories. For this to occur, a relationality of entries is essential. This implies that items within categories are not informational bits but are themselves categories organized in relation to other items subordinate to overarching frames.

The web of experiential knowledge is likely to consist of widely-distributed overlapping configurations such that excitement of even one synapse in a distributed connectivity could arouse others that are in distant or habitual relation. The massive inter-connectivity – billions if not trillions of contacts – accounts for the novelty and generative quality of thought, as well as its arousal in the temporal lag of what appears to be direct perception, while persistent activation of the same nodes would result in repetitive activation unless vigorously resisted, or by accessing novelty through a lapse to (activation of) phases prior to outcomes. This entails a retreat from a dominant focus on the analytic endpoints of thought to its holistic antecedents, a withdrawal to phases of generality, the "pool of the creative unconscious", that generate innovative contents prior to rigid precision.

Memory and Truth

The measure of truth is its conformance with reality, which in turn is determined by reliable perception. Only a fraction of perceptual experience can be framed as truth-judgments, for by far the greater part of our perceptions pass before us without thinking or remembering them. Presently, I see and hear such and such things in my garden. I can say it is true that the bush exists, and that it is green and flowerless, but such truths do not capture the totality of perceptual experience; other plants in the vicinity, the warmth and sunshine, the grass and gravel, the songs of the birds, the "chamber music" of summer insects, the furniture, the shadows and the breeze, my mood, my position and perspective and a myriad of other details, all of which are changing each moment. A memory is not a photograph but an approximation that revives ambient or less-noticed features of the original perception. Should I recall this experience much later, it is likely this moment would merge with others to give a generalized remembrance of similar moments condensed in a category and recalled as a collective. For example, a well-traveled route that, save for an unusual incident is remembered (known) without a unique memory of each occasion. The episodic fact tends to dissolve in the generality of its occurrence.

In sum, memory is not precisely true to experience, but its accuracy depends on perceptual revival. To the extent it strays from exactness it is thought, which incorporates pre-perceptual concepts but deviates from veridicality. A memory constrained by reality to realize an object world is a perception. An incompletely revived perception is a memory. The same ground of personal and impersonal knowledge gives rise to thought and memory, which are distinguished, *inter alia*, by a relation to events and the exactitude of reproduction. The world develops out of memory (thought), while phases in perception that do not externalize (antecedents in perception are intra-psychic) are memories or thoughts. Memories that are relatively veridical and with little thought content, such as eidetic images, fade to memory images. If perception actualizes prior to externalization the outcome is dream. If a recollection is about the experience from which it arises, it constitutes a memory. If it is about the objects to which it is directed it constitutes belief. To the extent concepts are uncoupled from objects, they constitute thought or imagination, and if they are impersonal and form a logical sequence, they constitute reason. The difference of thought, belief, reason and imagination can be attributed to their distance from actuality and reproduction, yet all these phenomena have a common ground in perceptual knowledge. The end of cognitive specification is the individuation of external objects out of thought, to which, to a varying degree, other mental phenomena aspire.

Appendix

Microgenesis and the Mind/Brain State: Interviews with Jason Brown

Jason W. Brown and David T. Bradford

Early Influences

David Bradford (DB): Major scientific projects often have a guiding metaphor which shapes the work and serves implicitly as a measure of adequacy. Were there certain images or metaphors that influenced your work from its very beginning, Jason?

Jason Brown (JB): Yes, there is one: a tree or a fountain, understood as the recurrent generation of form, as compared with a river, which portrays time as flowing. These metaphors have been in my mind since the earliest days. I could say now, years later, that the root is the "core self", the branch is the "concept", and the leaf is the "object".

DB: Root, branch, and leaf represent progressive degrees of differentiation. A fountain's water rises from a single source to traverse a given set of paths. Both the tree and fountain imply recursion with small adjustments. A river carries novel objects, always in one direction. These metaphors turn on different conceptions of time and change. Was there a particular source for your interest in time and the manner in which it brings about change?

JB: A source of which I am very much aware was Bergson and his work on pure duration. He does not have recurrence as a prominent theme, but he does have the notion of time as a point rather than a continuum. By contrast, the conventional way of thinking about (subjective) time is to stand above and see it as a line in space rather than a point that recurs. He also viewed perception as an active, productive process which contrasts with the passive in-processing account in neuroscience at that time and up to the present day. I read Bergson as a teenager and I think somehow these ideas were percolating in the shadows as I began my medical studies. I drifted quite far and did not return to this topic until many years later when I began to study psychology and brain function, starting with work on aphasia, a disturbance of the comprehension and formulation of language correlated with dysfunction in specific brain regions.

DB: What scientific work infuenced your early aphasia studies?

JB: One early influence was Paul Weiss, in embryology, who wrote about plasticity and specification; and there were others who had the idea of progressive specification, of individuation or differentiation, rather than accumulation or aggregation. Instead of aggregation or combination as the manner of formation, the idea of wholes that specified into parts was also a guiding metaphor. The metaphor of depth-and-surface was there, too, beginning with Freud's topographic theory, his metapsychology, the work on symptom formation and the transition from unconscious to conscious. Hughlings Jackson, in neurology, had similar ideas. There were several sources in evolutionary biology, people like Herrick, not well known today, and Jennings on the idea of an archetypal or iconic form that is transmuted in different organisms.

Another important influence on my studies of aphasia was the work of Arnold Pick, some of whose writings I had translated into English. Pick had a genetic model of language production, in which an utterance is realized over stages. Paul Schilder also took this approach in neuropsychology, postulating a succession of stages in the realization of an utterance. His paper on the Development of Thought was critical in my early years. Along with David Rapaport, and Henri Ey, he might be considered the father of a genetic school in psychoanalysis, in which a qualitative development from unconscious to conscious replaced the various interpretations of how ideas become conscious in Freudian orthodoxy.

DB: And how did you get concretely involved with your own work?

JB: None of the ideas just mentioned were formulated in any systematic way, but they were lodged somewhere in memory and framed the way I approached the work that followed on aphasia. I was well prepared for my year in Boston with Norman Geschwind. I had been reading extensively on aphasia and was in the process of writing a book on the topic when I came to Boston.

However, instead of developing separate models for dfferent phenomena, I tried to explain as much as I could in terms of an underlying framework. I also tried to incorporate a range of observations as arguments for the model, as if its explanatory power derived from its breadth; and to show, or at least prove to myself, that the model was general, authentic, and consistent across the many psychopathological disorders.

DB: Aphasia was your earliest testing ground. You then turned to other functional areas.

JB: As the model took shape, it became apparent to me that it was also applicable to the apraxias, or disorders of action-development, as well as to the agnosias, the disorders of perception that account for deviations in object-development. But the aphasia studies were, and still are in some respects, the doorway to neuropsychology.

DB: And the formulation of a comprehensive theory moved forward continuously.

JB: Yes, continuously but slowly. As you know, the history of aphasia is the history of progressive localization, leading from the phrenologists to Broca, who was as much the last of the phrenologists as the first of the aphasiologists. This led to more precise descriptions and localizations of part-functions and finally to functional modules, columns, and grandmother cells. Those who protested – the holists – did not have an alternative model; as Rapaport said in a different context, they were ministers without portfolios, critiques without solutions. The problem was to organize the aphasia symptoms in a theory that was consistent within a given domain of functions and across different aspects of language performance, both normal and pathological. The task was to see language perception and production from a unitary standpoint.

When it became clear that the posterior aphasias, which were considered problems in both production and perception, and the anterior aphasias, which were thought of as production disorders, could be understood in terms of a common processing sequence, this allowed me to meld perception and production into a common system. This goes back to Bergson's active or productive theory of perception.

DB: Holistic accounts were unwelcome or ignored when you began the aphasia studies. Why was that?

JB: Consider the history. The standard theory goes back to Meynert and Flechsig. This was the basis for the earliest schemas of aphasia and the basic outline that has guided thinking on the topic ever since. It is important to stress that the early history of aphasia is also the history of neuropsychology. Since language has been the most localizable function of the brain, the thinking was that if one could not localize language, forget about localizing everything else. Certain conditions like word deafness and auditory agnosias were interpreted as defects at different points in the processing of auditory information. The auditory or the visual signal was thought to arrive at the primary areas, then on to secondary and tertiary areas, and to association cortex.

In this view, there is a linear progression to more complex and multimodal areas by way of association pathways. The secondary and tertiary areas served for "higher" processing and the combining or assembling of sensory data.

It was common knowledge that the association or integration cortex in the frontal and parietal regions had undergone the greatest growth in the evolutionary sequence leading to man, and so they were naturally treated as the highest regions of the brain mediating the most complex modes of human thought. But this way of thinking was a fundamental error.

DB: … because it was not holistic enough?

JB: More than that, there were anatomical difficulties relating to the standard model of neocortical in-processing. For example, work by Bishop and Sanides showed that primary cortices were more recent in evolution than association or integration cortices, so if the direction of the cognitive process had anything to do with evolutionary process there should be a mapping of the evolutionary pattern of forebrain growth to the pattern of realization in language perception and production.

What prevented researchers from considering this idea was the computer model of the brain. Here, both the substrate and the sequence of manufacture were presumed to be unrelated to function, so the anatomical substrates of language were seen as secondary to the theory of language. The idea of input and output mechanisms reduced the complexity of perception and action systems to a sensory and motor apparatus.

In this view, the brain was conceived as a fixed structure, like a radio or television set, now a computer, and the mind as something that overlaid this structure or was discharged through it, like software driving the brain machinery. This was clearly not a dynamic system.

The introduction of evolutionary anatomy and the idea that cerebral growth persisted in patterns of cognitive function offered a dynamic perspective on prevailing structure, but the field was not ready for such a paradigm shift. Moreover, the details of the new concept still had to be worked out. In the early days of my aphasia work, I could only attempt to develop from the pathological material a concept of normal and pathological language and map this system onto evolutionary stages in the brain.

DB: So, summarizing all this, your theory differed from established views on several counts. Linguistic process was viewed as exclusively neocortical and advancing in a point-to-point fashion from primary areas to "higher" centers. The understanding of structure was neutral with respect to evolutionary and morphological development. This outlook lends itself to later computer analogies in which structure is analogous to hardware, and cognitive process is viewed as software which runs without intrinsic links with structure. The localization theory of the time laid the groundwork for the modularity of later cognitive neuropsychology. You were intent on understanding language and later perception and action as expression of a single process whose pattern of activation accorded with the growth planes of brain development.

JB: Yes, David, this is exactly right. And the work of Sanides was important to me, not as a basis for my own thinking but as an affirmation of my heading in the right direction from an anatomical standpoint. Another anatomist who offered support was Dee Pandya. Dee was a closet Sanidesian, so to say, with an evolutionary way of thinking. He encouraged me to pursue the path that I was on, a quite radical path, in which the primary areas were conceived, not as the initial sites in the reception of sense data which are then assembled into more complex entities but as termini of the bottom-up actualization.

At the time, there was only one theory of brain and language, and that was the old model of centers and pathways. I studied this with my first teacher, Johannes Neilson in California, the leading expert of his day on aphasia. He was thought to be a "localizer", but his work was subtler than is commonly believed. My next teacher, Norman Geschwind, was a true believer in the static model of the brain, in which language functions were deposited in bins and boxes. In this model, it was impossible to map to a dynamic neurology, much less to a dynamic theory of cognition. When it dawned on me that one could explain the posterior aphasias in terms of levels of perception which correspond with levels of action production, this opened the way for a unified theory. Many thought at the time, and still do, that language is put together in the back of the brain and sent to the frontal lobes for speech. The idea of a simultaneous development bottom up, from the archaic to the recent in evolutionary structure – a posterior system for language perception, an anterior system for production – was so far outside the usual paradigm that it did not receive much attention in the aphasia community. I was certain that language did not spring *de novo* from a genetic mutation but was grafted on perceptual and action systems inherited from our animal ancestry.

DB: After all, one of the major deficits of psychology and cognitive science until today is their lack of a consistent overarching theory. Your work in neuropathology was guided by the impulse to move toward such a theory.

JB: Yes, though the initial stages of synthesis occurred without full conscious attention. I recall William James, who wrote, probably in his essay on Fechner, that philosophy is not so much a matter of logic as of vision, the logic coming afterward to fill in the vision. So there was this idea, and then I looked for evidence in order to document it, to confirm it, to work it out.

Evolutionary Principles in Microgenesis

DB: As you indicated at various points before, the principles operative in mental process resemble those active in evolution. For example, as selection pressures determine physical adaptations, so sensory constraints shape object-formation, doing so on a moment-by-moment basis. This is one example. The comparison of evolutionary and microgenetic theories plays a significant role in your approach.

JB: Darwin had certain basic principles in his theory of evolution into which he collapsed the diversity of life forms; survival of the fittest, selection pressure, and adaptation to the environment are the main examples. My way of thinking has been similar: to understand the diversity of pathological forms by means of a few underlying principles.

As it turns out, they are evolutionary principles similar to the Darwinian idea of natural selection and competition among organisms. The concept of sensory constraints on object-formation corresponds with the elimination of the unfit. The environment in the form of sensation trims the potential for a diversity of objects to those that conform to the external world. The objects before us are momentary adaptations that have "competed" for survival during the final phases of the object-formation.

The evolutionary theme plays out in the micro-temporal process of the unfolding of thought, act, object, and utterance. A person without natural constraints on object-formation has an illusory or hallucinatory world, and will be, or soon become, psychotic, perhaps placed in an institution where his fictitious perceptions will not subject him to risk.

DB: We are moving quickly. The mental state is central in microgenetic theory. Its synonyms include "cognitive epoch" or "mind/brain state". "Micro-temporal" process refers to the state's composition and temporal characteristics. A series of phases or transitions activates neural structure from brainstem forward, subjecting content to a series of qualitative changes. Pathology impedes or truncates transitions, and the result is symptoms. In later writings, you say the state constitutes the basic unit of time. This is a difficult topic which overlaps with ideas in process philosophy and the Buddhist theory of nowness. But let us first stay with evolutionary principles in microgenetic theory.

JB: While phylogenesis refers to a population dynamic in the derivation of species, microgenesis is a theory of the specification of an endogenous act or image in a single individual. Phylogenesis occurs over millions of years, microgenesis in a fraction of a second. In evolution, there is excessive or exuberant production of organisms. Many more are born than will survive, and those that do survive must live long enough to reproduce through competitive interaction. This compares with object-formation in microgenesis. Its earliest phase is that of a potential for the development of many different objects, images, dream-like forms. There are intrinsic constraints such as habit and the just-preceding state, and the extrinsic constraints of sensation that limit the possible routes of development. In evolution, the less fit, or less lucky, organisms die in the world, though anomalies can die stillborn. In microgenesis, objects "die" or remain unrealized, as others take their place. At successive phases, the forming pre-object is subjected to continuous sculpting, trimming, and parsing. In other words, a continuous partition of the developing configuration underlies the final outcome.

DB: All of which is pre-conscious.

JB: Yes, preconscious. But there are also constraints at the final phase of consciousness. This could be interpreted, in agreement with Libet's work, as a veto on final action. The difference is that we are conscious of the final veto, or constraint, not of the constraints active in antecedent phases. These are unconscious. It is not that volition acts at the terminus of the development to sculpt the final act. Rather, we are just aware of the potential for sculpting when the microgenesis passes through those segments that give rise to choice or decision.

DB: Decision-making amounts to the negation of an imminent possibility. There is no unboundedly free agent in microgenesis, although the feeling of agency accompanies thoughts and actions as they pass into conscious awareness. Amid the preconscious proliferation and the largely automatic suppression of competing possibilities, is there room for choice? And to what degree is it conscious?

JB: We have the opportunity to develop images, thoughts, or pre-actions in the sense of an implicit choice at each phase. By implicit I mean unaware. The choice or selection is carried on to the next phase, where it is transformed into something else. The process has a fractal-like quality, except that the transform is qualitative, not a sequence of self-similar representations.

When a choice becomes explicit, or conscious, and open to introspection, this gives the feeling that we are making conscious decisions. Whether or not we make conscious decisions or are instead informed of decisions that have already occurred is another issue, but the becoming-conscious of implicit choice is part of the feeling of agency and decision. It is important to see that, in microgenetic theory, introspection is a coming-to-the-fore of earlier phases in the actualization process, not an addition to the cognitive process.

Incidentally, the notion that consciousness of mental content, introspection, is not appended to the mental state but emerges at a penultimate phase in its development and is consistent with the evolutionary principle that new form arises at earlier, less specialized stages, not by terminal addition.

DB: Early on, evolutionary principles were seen to be active in microgenesis; then afterward, you incorporated new information about brain-related changes during fetal and later development.

JB: Well, I incorporated work in morphogenesis, specifically sculpting and parcellation. Papers on parcellation were appearing in the late 1980s, and this concept helped me to see the ontogenetic dimension in morphogenesis. This had previously eluded me, since microgenetic phases were mapped to phylogenetic growth planes without including ontogeny. In the development of the embryonic brain during fetal life, many more cells are produced than survive, and many more connections. It has been shown, for example in macaque, that trillions of connections are lost in the post-fetal growth of the primate forebrain.

This demonstrates that selectivity is achieved by the elimination of cells and connections. In cognition, specificity is achieved by the inhibition of established connections, and then, by a selective individuation leading from potentiality to actuality. More precisely, the elimination of cells and connections in morphogenesis continues in cognitive development by way of inhibition, which accomplishes much the same thing as elimination of connections. The transition from elimination to inhibition then continues as the constraints on the process of actualization, which account for the individuation of parts out of antecedent wholes.

I see this as a cascade of context-item shifts. The point is that the patterns of embryonic growth lay down the patterns of the cognitive process. Morphogenesis does not just give us a brain that outputs function. Instead, the lines of fetal growth continue into maturity as the lines of cognitive process. One could say that specification by the elimination of cells and connections in early life becomes specification by inhibition of established connections, and also the inhibition, or transformation by constraints, as the cognitive process develops over evolutionary layers. Process is four-dimensional growth. Early in life, form is laid down in the form of morphology. Later, form is laid down in the form of behavior. A single process underlies structure and function.

DB: We are now talking about extended analogies between three kinds of change. The first is evolutionary change; the second is ontogenesis and the developmental changes of morphogenesis; the third is microgenesis. Each has its respective time frame, ranging from very long periods of time in the case of evolution, to months and years in the case of the individual organism, to the fraction of a second required for the completion of individual mental states. All are subject to comparable patterns of change, which are called "process". The joint emphasis on process shows how the kinds of change are alike.

JB: In evolution, speciation occurs over millions of years. The cat that rubs its back against my leg is the same kind of cat that rubbed its back a thousand years ago. The same cat over and over, like transformations with some novelty over evolutionary time. The growth, death, and replacement of organisms occurs as a cyclical process spread out over the lifespan, while the arising, perishing, and re-birth of a cognition occurs in a fraction of a second as an epoch of change that replaces itself.

But the cyclical nature of replacement differs from the historical nature of a linear concatenation or causal chain of events.There is also a conflict between the cyclical time of a recurrence model and the linear time of a causal model. It is rather like the tide that surges and withdraws and surges once again, or like the seasons that come and go. Later, I became aware that the concept of the arising and perishing of a temporal present, the mental state, was linked to certain traditions in Indian philosophy as well as to process metaphysics.

DB: We return to Bergson and his idea of time as a recurring point.

JB: Well, Bergson was important to me in other ways too. For one thing, he described perception as active, not a passive input. And, more practically speaking, he also wrote that time given to disputation is time lost. Disputation was not something I wanted to expend energy on, especially since the criticism of the holists has been their lack of an alternative approach that is respectful of the detail. My primary concern was the effort to develop an alternative model. However, working in the context of cognitive psychology, even participating actively in many seminars and conferences during the birth pangs of this new field, it was difficult to avoid taking into consideration the cognitivist perspective and seeing my work as one in opposition.

Yet, I would not say the work developed out of opposition to cognitive science, or to localization approaches in neuropsychology. It rather took on shape naturally on its own, though many of the conceptual problems required confronting strongly entrenched views in both of these overlapping fields. Still, there was a rather hostile environment, and I well recall the many arguments, even the ridicule, at many scientific meetings. I didn't even find a receptive environment in the school of my former teachers, Johannes Nielsen, Norman Geschwind, and Alexander R. Luria. In fact, after the passing of these neurologists, localization theory evolved to an even more virulent modularity.

DB: Which continues to this day.

JB: Yes, and with the semblance of a science offered by neuro-imaging techniques, it is becoming still more pervasive, making it much more difficult to sustain a holistic view, as well as to convince others of its importance. One can challenge modularity on many grounds, as I have. The flow diagrams and circuit boards do not correlate with psychological reality but are a facile means of resolving local findings without an overarching framework. The recent impact of "binding" theory is a good example of an attempt, purely artificial, to tie together the multiplicity of anatomical and functional elements, which have been separated in the trend to ever finer analysis, by an improvised external linkage.

At some point, I realized the futility of argument against the tide of research and decided to dedicate myself to exploring the theory as deeply and widely as possible. In some ways, the progression has been similar to that of Freud, whose theory, having gone through various forms, was extended to literature, religion, and social concepts.

DB: Your book *Process and the Authentic Life* does precisely this. In particular, it focuses on the expressions and neuropsychological formation of value. What stimulated your interest in the matter of value?

JB: I think my interest in value began with a paper on aesthetic perception. This had to do with the idea that one does not see an object and then think about it as a separate phenomenon, though this looks like a natural assumption. In microgenetic theory, one thinks up the object, the object is a thought product. A great deal of thought goes on unconsciously, implicitly, and evanescently in perceiving the object. When you see a chair, you know it is a chair. You have a history of encounters with chairs or chair-like objects and the relations of chairs to other kinds of furniture; the richness of the underlying category "furniture" is the background of the perceived chair.

When one thinks about an object, thought is not added to the object. What happens is that you withdraw to preliminary phases in the original object-formation, phases that are more thought-like, less object-like. You retreat into the infrastructure of the object and explore its depth. Thought is kind of an archeology of perception since objects are externalized concepts, their objectifications as it were, while object-concepts are themselves realizations of yet deeper categories.

It is categories all the way down, so to say, as the Buddhists have argued, and I would as well. So, on this way of thinking, aesthetic perception is not an interpretation added to a perception, say the interpretation of a painting or a piece of music, but an exploration of the underpinnings of the original object. The exploration furthers a growth of the concept through metaphoric and other mechanisms.

DB: But isn't this quite counter-intuitive? The common-sense idea is that we see an object, any object, or a work of art, and we think about it, rather than that the object grows out of thought.

JB: This growing out is reenacted and captured in artistic creation. The artist creates the object the aesthete enjoys, but the latter also creates the object with greater or lesser depth. The object is not an independent thing in the world. Subsequent observation and thought on the object yields the infra-structure of the original perception. This approach to aesthetics led me to think about drive, desire, and other feelings, including moral feeling, that are also preliminary in the derivation of objects. The microgenetic idea is that feeling accompanies the pre-object outward in its trajectory from mind to world, from the core of the mind to its surface. In my theory, the world is the external rim of the mind. Feeling travels outward as part of the object and inhabits the object as interest, worth, or value. We do not see an object and add the feeling but revive the earlier psychic segments of the configuration from which feeling trickled into the externalized object.

DB: Now we are talking about feeling, which – if I remember correctly – was outside our discussion so far.

JB: Let me say that thinking about feeling or emotion created a very interesting new problem for me. Those who study concepts, objects, or language tend to separate them from emotion. Certainly, cognitive psychology and much of prior psychology tended to ignore emotion. Even William James, in his theory with Lange, thought of emotion as a kind of peripheral phenomenon, with emotions attached to thoughts. This is also the case with Freud's concept of cathexis. I could not understand how a thought called up a feeling, or a feeling lured the appropriate thought.

The problem was how feelings and ideas come together, and it did not seem to me that they actually did come together. Rather, they were fused from the start in what one could call, after Freud, a drive representation, or an archaic categorical primitive invested with an affective tonality. I referred to this togetherness of concept and feeling simply as "conceptual feeling" which individuates into what appear to be discrete concepts and feelings, though even the most abstract concepts have a feeling tone and the most primitive feelings devolve out of categories.

It was natural for me to think of a drive-like construct individuating into partial affects and partial concepts, then into lexical and object concepts, and action plans, each having a feeling tone. The feeling can become exaggerated at the expense of the concept, and the concept can become so dry or abstract it seems drained of feeling, but they trace to an earlier phase where the concept and feeling are part of the same entity.

DB: I like this definition of a conceptual feeling: a categorical primitive invested with affective tonality. You mention Freud – a closer analogy is Jung's theory of the complex. An archetypal structure organizes its content and amplifies its emotional power; in this sense, the complex is like a categorical primitive.

JB: To anticipate, I later came to see the feeling as the becoming, and the concept or object as the being, of the same entity. The feeling is the process, the concept is the substance. In a way, feeling travels with the object into the world and is part of the object. In microgenetic theory, the object is not merely the endpoint of the process, as a product on a conveyor belt, nor the output of the earlier phases, but the entire epoch from bottom to top. An object and the world of which it is a part is the whole cognition that includes the early phases through which it has been derived.

DB: The point you were just now emphasizing is that object-formation is inherently emotional, and the same would apply to thought and action.

JB: Yes, emotional. The idea that one has a naked object to which feeling or interpretation is added seemed odd to me, since in microgenetic theory all of that was subsumed within the original perception. This under-surface is not apparent to the observer, and so what the observer has to do is delve back into the formative phases in the pre-history of the perception. As you said before, this is quite counter-intuitive!

DB: I suspect it's also a matter of personal temperament how counter-intuitive these ideas seem. Introversion inclines attention to preliminary phases of object-formation, which may have a salience comparable to fully differentiated objects. Persons trained in certain forms of meditation would experience directly the rising formation of objects in preliminary phases preceding their assumption of definite form and meaning in fully conscious awareness. I suppose these ideas are most counterintuitive for extroverted individuals with relatively little capacity for introspection. Obviously, they are counter-intuitive for the common-sense view that things appear whole-cloth without trailing the residue of earlier cognitive formation.

JB: Coming back to the problem with aesthetic perception: This problem was not, as some analytical thinkers argued, that of applying interpretations to objects but to access the unconscious richness of what is already there. This is related to the microgenetic concept of memory, where an object, as it develops into the world, passes from long-term through short-term memory to perception. The different phases in object perception are the different stages in memory. It is not as if you see something which is then conveyed to short-term and long-term memory but rather the reverse. It develops out of long-term memory, out of the past, through short-term memory, closer to the now, and finally into a present object. The direction of microgenesis is from unconscious to conscious, from depth to surface, from self to world, and from past to present. So, the object actually brings the past into the present.

DB: Long-term memory draws on the category that prompts the immediate perception of a given chair.

JB: Yes. But the perception of a chair is also highly constrained by the sense data hitting the brain and conforming an endogenous and wholly intrinsic process to represent the chair.

DB: As if the sensory constraints pick and choose from memory.

JB: Essentially. Sensory constraints arising in brainstem bias early phases in perception in a certain direction. Subsequently, there is a relative suspension of sensory constraints on the developing object as it passes through the limbic system, a phase of personal or experiential memory and feeling. Then, sensation is again exerted on the terminal phase where the final featural details and externalization of the object occur. The object passes through a dream-like phase of personal memory and experience to final exteriorization and detachment as something independent in the world. In neuropathology, we see all these intermediate phases.

I was once asked by Francis Crick when I gave a paper on this topic:

"Why couldn't you just reverse the whole process? You know, instead of going bottom to top, just go top to bottom?" My answer was that it would be like reversing evolution, because the growth of an object or the growth of an utterance or an action follows an evolutionary pattern. Evolution is unidirectional, and so is microgenesis. The direction of cognition has to be that of evolutionary growth.

There are other reasons why the process is irreversible, but because the theory reverses the standard view of the direction of percept formation, it was unpalatable to many who research this area. Moreover, in computational psychology and the computer model of the brain, many would argue that it does not matter how you assemble a computer, which parts you put in first.

It is similar to the function of a car, which is unaffected if the carburetor is put in before or after the wheels. A brain as a machine is approached in the same way. The stage at which a certain structure appears in evolution was thought to be irrelevant to its function.

On my way of thinking, the evolutionary growth pattern is fundamental to the processing direction in cognition. Later, this idea led to the view that cognition and growth are the same process – that cognition is a mode of growth. Learning and forgetting are the evidence that cognition is a growth process, while behavior involves the dynamic in structure.

Microtemporal Structure of the Mind/Brain State

DB: Let's now talk about the internal structure of the mind/brain state and the sense of time that it entails. This involves consideration of the phases whose serial activation brings the state to the point of completion. If blocked or impeded, as occurs in pathological conditions, the series closes prematurely. Symptoms appear on this basis, and I would suspect that the sense of time is altered as well.

It seems to me that mental processes, under normal conditions, are highly unreliable in the sense that successive sets of states show great variability in their degrees of completeness. This would allow for rapid change in the form and content of consciousness. A person might alternate between attending to emotionally salient remote memories and the absent-minded effort of tallying the debits marked in his check register. Time seems to linger and pool during the reminiscence, but is quickened, uneven, and possibly races during a mathematical task. Another example would be trance-like immersion in hallucinatory imagery, alternating with objective awareness of the ambient environment. To shift from the clinical perspective, the field of religious studies provides an example in the experience of what seems a timeless duration, which the mystic interprets as participation in the eternal life of God.

You hold that neighboring states overlap. The lingering trace of the preceding state sculpts the next in sequence based on the earlier state's imposition of memory. This idea could be extended to account for the near-simultaneous presence of different levels of consciousness. The schizophrenic might listen to his voices while conversing with the hospital attendant. Attention lingers in preliminary, hallucinatory phases, meanwhile the mouth parrots ideas keyed to later phases. Rapid alternation between the two activities would give the impression of their simultaneous occurrence.

JB: These are interesting topics that touch on imagery, introspection, metaphor, and paralogical thinking. I suppose the alteration of timing or of the time sense in, say, melancholia has to do with the loss of objects, especially in severe depression. Many have written that the unconscious is timeless. Eduard von Hartmann was the first, I believe, then Zigmund Freud and Carl Gustav Jung. I don't think timeless entities can exist, so either the unconscious is not timeless or there are no unconscious entities. Apart from the hypothesis of abstract or eternal Platonic objects, existence is temporal.

I would prefer to say that events in the physical world, and also unconscious happenings, are simultaneous. One might question the distinction between simultaneity and timelessness, in supposing a lack of temporal order in the simultaneous instant. However, within a simultaneity, there is temporal extension, a transition of phases, or becoming, that does not achieve existence until the succession is complete and a single mental state actualizes. This is the difference between the simultaneous and the non-temporal. The simultaneous is potentially temporal but not without a complete epoch of transition. All entities, physical or mental, have a minimal duration over which one complete state is achieved.

The transition within an entity, say a tree in perception or a mental object such as an idea, is the succession from onset to termination that lays down one complete thing. This transition is replaced so rapidly that it is unapparent, and we are aware only of the final actuality, which seems to be a product of the processes on which it depends. In microgenetic theory, an entity or object is not a slice of process in time or the output of prior operations but the full sequence of antecedent phases.

The succession is not "in time" until it terminates and the full sequence is realized. This implies the temporal thickness that all objects or entities possess. In mind, it pertains especially to unconscious phenomena. When unconscious happenings transition to consciousness, they take on temporal order. Presumably, events that remain unconscious still achieve closure and replacement, though we cannot know such events until they become conscious. The dream, for example, in my view is simultaneous until one awakens when for a brief moment it is apprehended all at once in its entirety. In dream, there is no duration, just a present that is constantly replaced. It is only in retrospect, that one attempts to reconstruct the sequence in a narrative that makes sense to the waking subject.

DB: That's very interesting. It sounds as if the sequential narrative of a dream, which we conceive of temporally, is actually a projection into time of something pristinely embedded in simultaneity.

JB: The creation of temporal order articulates space and gives the succession of events in perception. It is important to distinguish the succession that underlies the perception of events from that which is perceived in the world. The one is real or genuine change that deposits a novel object; the other is apparent or illusory change that results from the replacement of objects, giving the appearance of an ordered series of events. This concept may be difficult to follow. The change we see in the world is illusory; the change we do not see inside an object is genuine and novel. In the replacement of each epoch, genuine change accounts for apparent change.

The question for the philosophical substantialist is how change occurs for "solid" objects; in other words, the nature of the causal step from one state to the next. The problem for process thinking is how flux divides into objects. From a process standpoint, objects are the illusory stabilities of events. The change within the object is invisible while the change across objects is an effect of the replacement of epochs. These concepts conflict with our common-sense view of things.

The feeling of duration requires a past and a present, not mere succession. Duration is bound up with a specious present hovering over the phase transition. The point is that a truncated becoming gives a contracted present. This occurs in severe amnesia, when event-decay is so rapid that unfilled durations shrink. For the amnesic, a month feels like days. An alteration of time accompanies an alteration of change. In meditation, the goal is to expand the now of present experience so it embraces all past and future time. And you are right: mystics such as Eckart and Coomaraswamy wrote of states in which the now approaches the eternal now of God's mind.

DB: I notice that you use terms like "transition" and "phase" but also the term "stratum" has some appeal because of the connotations of surface and depth, which support the idea that neural processing advances toward the forebrain, activating more deeply situated structures before coming to cortex. Can you briefly trace the course of transitions constituting a single state?

JB: As to terminology, I try to avoid "stratum", as I don't use "plane", "stage", "level".

DB: Why is that?

JB: The words suggest a more persistently defined, a more static idea than for instance "phase". Phase has a more dynamic quality. I speak of "phase" or a "phase transition" and of "segments" in the transition as a continuum that is arbitrarily demarcated. One has a kind of clustering at certain phases, but a phase does not usually appear, for it is transformed to an ensuing phase. An intermediate phase is observed as a momentary terminus when it actualizes as a dream image or, in pathology, as a symptom.

DB: I am beginning to doubt my previous understanding of these terms.

JB: David, to clarify, I think that a phase is unstable. It appears as a symptom, but in normal cognition, it is always transitional to an ensuing phase. When one phase transitions to the next, it vanishes, having given up what it *was* to what it *becomes*. I avoid terms such as "level", "stage", or "plane" to avoid the suggestion of stability in the phase. I use the term "phase transition" for the microgenetic sequence, and the term "segment" for some succession or series of phases within that sequence.

DB: I mentioned the idea that series of states may be highly inconsistent in their respective degrees of development and said this might account for the experience of nearly simultaneously carrying out different kinds of tasks, each keyed to a particular series of phases.

JB: You were speaking about multiple levels, or strata, of consciousness. I think the question is not whether one has multiple levels, or rather phases, but that one needs them, first to be conscious, which occurs when the phase of the self is aware of the phase of an object world. The self-object relation is a relation of early to late phases in the same mental state. Introspection is not an addition to the sequence but a branching from preliminary phases. It entails the coming-to-the-fore of phases between self and object. It is essential that the mental state terminates in a veridical object. Otherwise, introspective contents will undergo distortion in archaic modes of cognition, as occurs in dreams.

Dream is consciousness of an image world when the object-development is arrested. The difference between dream and waking consciousness is that in wakefulness an image occurs in relation to the self at one pole and an object at the other. Images close to waking consciousness tend to be "reality-oriented"; those more preliminary, as with reverie or fantasy, can be like dream-images. Verbal and visual imagery – inner speech, for example, and other forms of imagery – are interposed between the self and the outer world. The object- and activity-awareness that Piaget thought was typical of young children, perhaps of animals, is an immediacy of awareness, without mediation by a self. I speak of the relation of *subject to object* as "awareness", and the relation of *self to object* as "consciousness".

The self is not only conscious of objects, but of images in the context of a perception of the external world. There is also a volitional or intentional quality of the imagery. We feel that we are agents of inner speech, and that we control thought imagery. However, without an external world, an image becomes an actuality or endpoint, as in dream or hallucination. Moreover, the self of dream is a different self than in wakefulness. It is passive, swept along by events, without a sense of willing or guiding events. It is drawn by the events to which it is a witness or victim.

DB: Let me go back to the phase transition. "Transition" avoids the connotation of something fixed and for this reason is preferrable to "stratum" or "level". To grasp the unbroken continuity of the state's development is not an easy task. A temporal perspective has to be substituted for fixed points of reference. How would you describe in detail the passage of a single state whose outcome is the formation of a particular perceptual object?

JB: Let's say we are looking at a table. We have no sense of an underlying sequence of phases. We just see the table and we think we see it directly. How can we experience an antecedent sequence of phases that very rapidly delivers the table into consciousness?

Usually, we can't, but the phases are exposed in pathology. The disorders of object-perception reveal the microtemporal transitions that underlie external objects. In any event, there have to be antecedent phases, whether one thinks of them as assembling the object and projecting it outward or, as I do, individuating the object from a background potential. In either case, there are antecedent events from which the perception develops. These phases are imminent in the object.

In my view, the background is a cascade of whole-part transforms. When one looks at the separate aspects of an object – the color, the shape, the movement, and so on – it is natural to think there are mechanisms in the brain that mediate such features or properties. But in hallucination, one observes that object boundaries are really color boundaries or boundaries of hue. Without color, and without the achromatic colors, the world disappears. This happens in snow blindness. There is always some color boundary. In hallucination, colors melt off objects into a space that is like an object, a space that is viscous or palpable, not the empty space of normal perception.

DB: That sounds very much like what you said about dreams before.

JB: Yes, I think that in waking hallucination the same features as in dreams are perceived adjacent to normal objects in a separate locus of the visual field. In pathological cases, hallucinations may replace objects in the affected part of the visual field and are often the initial symptom of object loss. Auditory hallucinations replace or rather supplant auditory perceptions. These as well as many other clinical observations and studies indicate that images and perceptions are not served by different mechanisms, but rather images are attenuated objects or, conversely, objects result from sensory constraints applied to exteriorizing imagery.

One could say that perception develops out of an hallucinatory background. More precisely, the ground of the hallucination, not the image content but the phase mediating that content, is transformed by sensation to an external object. An hallucination is what happens to a pre-object, such as an image or a concept, when the final sensory sculpting is not applied. In brief, an object is an image, an hallucination, that is sculpted and so adapted by sensory data to the outside world.

When we withdraw from objects to images, we encounter a variety of image types, each accompanied by a different sense of self and agency. We feel that we search for a memory image; we try to recall a memory and are frustrated if we can't remember it. Hallucinations in pathology or hypnagogy come to us without warning or control. If we reach for an hallucination, it may disappear. In hypnagogic states, which are marvelous to behold – usually faces more brilliant than life, colorful, agonized – one tries to be passive and let the experience continue, but as soon as the eyes are diverted to the image or one reaches for it, the image disappears. To hold it, one must remain a passive spectator like the self in dream.

Actually, the passivity of the dream self is important because I think it explains paranoid ideation, where one has the feeling of being a victim of one's own imagery. Images can even take on a kind of agency of their own, as in command hallucination, where verbal hallucinations instruct the person what to do. The sense of personal agency is lost, or transferred to the image. This, by the way, shows that the feeling of agency or volition is not standing behind the content but develops and changes with the momentary state.

DB: So now we are coming back to agency, volition, and willful action, and their various kinds of impairments. This seems to be a much more subtle picture than flatly declaring free will an illusion.

JB: Normally, we don't feel an agent to objects. They are happenings out there in the world that impinge on us. We do have a sense of agency when we imagine a mouse crawling over the back of an elephant. There is a sense of volition in visual imagery. We can call up the imagined sound of music or a conversation. Volition is not just linked to action; it is also woven into the antecedents of perception. In eidetic imagery, there is some feeling of voluntary control. As eidetic images decay to memory images, the sense of volition changes.

The feeling of volition depends on the dominant phase in the transition, which is associated with different forms of imagery. From this, one can reconstruct the sequence of object- or image-formation, as well as that of object-concept, meaning, and feeling. What I mean by this is that images differ in their meaning-content. Dreams are symbolic images that we feel the need to interpret. Hypnagogic images are filled with affect. Eidetic images are pictorial and appear relatively meaning-free. Memory images can have profound meaning for the individual. The way these different images are related to successive phases in the object-formation – from conceptual feeling to object value, from an archaic to a rational mentation, as well as from past to present or mind to world – reveals the transition from deep phases of categorical primitives associated with drive-like affect to meaning-laden, intentional concepts and images, and finally to world-close configurations achieving mind-independence …

DB: … which can never be perfectly independent, because of the series of antecedents from which each emerges.

JB: Yes! As one goes more deeply into the precursors of external objects, one accesses the intense feeling of drive. At the other pole of the mental state, an object in the world seems free of personal affect, or it seems to have an affect of its own, initially its existence, than its worth or value. There is feeling in the object; rather, objects are filled with our own feeling that travels with them from the mind. We sense this when we love someone, or desire an object, and the object becomes the focus of attention.

In this sense, interest or focal attention is the first sign of value. We see a face in a crowd, we notice it and have some interest in that face. The face takes on greater value than other faces. Gradually, the personality behind the face grows in significance. As we get to know the person, our affection can develop into love. The face of the beloved then fills the entire field, soaks up all of the feeling that was distributed before. Feeling is now concentrated in one object of overwhelming desire. The same applies in the case of other emotions such as fear and hate. They all signal the presence of value.

Emotion becomes intense and is felt in both ourselves and the object. Often, we have the experience of not knowing whether the feeling is in the object or in the self. Is she beautiful because we love her, or do we love her because she is beautiful? Do I desire this diamond because it is valuable, or is its value raised by my desire? We don't know if desire creates the feeling in and for the object or if feeling in the object provokes the desire.

I think this shows that the boundary between self and object, mind and world, is artificial. It also shows that value is a complex phenomenon, with an unconscious core, a conscious desire, and a worth that seems located in the object. The fragile boundary between mind and world is evident in psychosis as thoughts become like objects and objects become thought-like. The psychotic has the insight of a continuous transition from mind to world, which the normal person has lost.

DB: Incipient value is a basic mark of the object's existence. In accruing feeling, it draws and holds attention and assumes focal importance. Once feeling is supplied to the object, mental process is already set in motion.

JB: A major preoccupation in all my work has been the subject-object relation. Whether the relationship is framed in terms of self and

> other, or Buber's "I" and "Thou", it has played a major part in many different approaches to neuropsychology and philosophy.

In my own work, the nature of the self and the relation of self to other is treated in a subjectivist way. I argue that feeling goes from self to object, that feeling in an object passes into it from the self. Thus, when one begins to fall in love, the self creates the other as a receptacle for its own feeling, which arises in the core and empirical self, flows into desire and then trickles into the value and interest of the beloved's face. Whether value or interest in the other strengthens or weakens depends on the self-concept, our needs, core values, and beliefs.

Essentially, what I tried to work out is how the other is a self-creation. The common-sense idea that we meet a person, get to know each other and gradually, through external contacts, feeling develops, is the usual way of thinking about this experience. For me, it is backward. Microgenesis is a counter-intuitive theory. It holds that the other is a creation of the self, that the other comes to fill a larger or smaller portion of one's own self-concept, and that in order to know the other one has to withdraw into one's own self more deeply to find a common ground in which antecedents of the self and the other cohabitate, a potential out of which both are realized.

The ground that gives rise to the self and the other is beneath my consciousness and that of the other person. I imagine self and other to be part of a deeper unity that has to be accessed in a descent through many, many internal phases.

Glossary

Ab origo Earliest beginning; lineage origin. *Lat.* - "from the beginning"
Agnosia Inability to recognise objects
Aktualgenese *See microgenesis*
Anhedonia Inability to feel pleasure in normally pleasurable activities
Antecedent phases Phases that come before others
Aphasia Language disorder caused by damage to a specific area of the brain that mediates language expression and communication
Apraxia Inability to carry out motor actions in spite of normal function
Bauplan Underlying structural plan
Brain morphology Pertaining to structural measures of the brain (volume, shape organisation)
Cathexis The energy invested in a mental entity
Concrescence A word invented by A.N. Whitehead to express the idea of something fluid in the process of becoming concrete
Cogito The philosophical principle that one's existence is demonstrated by the fact that one thinks. The root-category for rationalist accounts of understanding as achievable by eliminating doubt
Cognitivism An approach which aims to understand the mind by comparing it to an information-processing device like a computer
Deconstruction A type of philosophical activity popularised by Jacques Derrida which involves showing how concepts which seem natural are actually constructed
Diachronic change from antecedent to consequent
Dialetics A unity and evolution of opposites which leads to growth, development or novelty when they do not exclude (or do not eliminate) each other. The art of investigating or discussing the truth of opinions.
Diaschisis Release or compensation by neighbouring or contralateral regions in the brain
Eidetic Relating to or denoting mental images in relation to perception, having unusual vividness and detail as if actually visible
Eliminative materialism The doctrine that more complex processes like communication and consciousness can be reduced without loss to material processes

Epigenetic mechanisms Refers to mechanisms that translate the genetic code into morphology

Epiphenomenal A secondary symptom occurring simultaneously as a disease or condition but not directly related to it; a mental state as a by-product of brain activity

Epistemology The study of knowledge and what it means to know

Hemianopia Loss of vision in a visual field

Heterochrony The development of cells or tissues at an abnormal time relative to other unaffected events in an organism

Homo *Sapiens* The scientific name for human beings

Hypnagogic Relating to the state immediately before falling asleep

Innervationsgefuhle The feeling that accompanies a motor action

Inter alia Amongst other things

Lacuna A cavity or depression, especially in bone. In philosophy – a lack in further explanation, missed argument

Localisation The endeavour to situate particular brain functions in particular regions of the brain

Magnum Opus Main work

Microgenesis The development of a mind/brain state within a brief present-time scale

Mind/brain state A formulation designed to emphasise the inseperable togetherness of brain states and states of mind

Morphogenesis A biological process that causes a tissue or organ to develop its shape by controlling the spatial distribution of cells during embryonic development

Morphological Pertaining to the structure or form of an entity

Motoric Processes in the central nervous system concerned with the production of actions

Neoteny The retention of juvenile features in the adult animal

Noumenon Knowledge posited as an object that exists independently of human sense. Generally used in contrast to or in relation to the term phenomenon which refers to any object of the senses

Ontogenesis The process of an individual organism growing organically

Ontology The study of what it means to exist. A section in philosophy that focused on being as category and reality

Panprotopsychism The doctrine that fundamental physical entities while not themselves minded have special features that give rise to conscious minds when they are arranged into a sufficiently complex physical system

Parsing Resolving something into its component parts

Phylogenesis The evolutionary development and diversification of a species or group of organisms; or of a particular feature of an organism

Prosodic Contour The set of prosodic features other than voice quality, i.e., intensity, fundamental frequency, speech rate and rhythm

Prosopagnosia Inability to recognise faces

Qualia The essential mental states corresponding to experiences (what we feel in perception, empirically, e.g., reddness, pain, etc.)

Sociogenesis The becoming of society

Subjectivity The condition of being a subject: one that goes through an experience

Tabula rasa The idea that when people are born their mind is effectively a blank slate, their experiences make them who they are

Tropism The orientation of an organism in a direction responsive to an external stimulus.

Bibliography

Anscombe, G. E. M. (1963). *Intention.* Second edition. Oxford: Blackwell.

Arkin, A. and Brown, J. (1971). *Aphasic speech, schizophrenic speech, sleep speech and sleep-talking.* Bruges, Belgium: Association of psychophysiological study of sleep.

Atmanspacher, H. and Filk, T. (2011). Contra classical causality. *Journal of Consciousness Studies, 19*, 95–116.

Bergson, H. (1922). *Durée et simultanéité*. Paris: Félix Alcan.

Bernstein, N. (1967). *The coordination and regulation of movements.* London: Pergamon.

Bortolotti, L. (2022). *Delusion, The Stanford encyclopedia of philosophy.* Stanford University. https://plato.stanford.edu/archives/sum2022/entries/delusion/.

Brown, J.W. (1972). *Aphasia, apraxia and agnosia.* Springfield, IL: Thomas.

Brown, J.W. (1977). *Mind, Brain and consciousness.* New York: Academic Press.

Brown, J. W. (1978). Lateralization: A brain model. *Brain and Language*, *5*, 258–261.

Brown, J. W. (1988). *Life of the mind.* Hillsdale, NJ: Erlbaum.

Brown, J. W. (1989). Neuropsychology of visual perception perception, Institute for research in behavioral neuroscience. Erlbaum: Psychology press.

Brown, J. W. (1991). *Self and process.* New York: Springer-Verlag.

Brown, J. W. (1994). Morphogenesis and mental process. *Development and Psychopathology*, *6*, 551–563.

Brown, J. W. (1996). *Time, will and mental process.* New York: Plenum.

Brown, J. W. (2000). *Mind and nature. Essays on time and subjectivity.* London: Whurr Publishers.

Brown, J. W. (2002). *The self-embodying mind.* Barrytown, New York: Station Hill Press.

Brown, J. W. (2004). A microgenetic approach to time and memory in neuropsychology. *Acta Neuropsychologica*, *2*(1), 1–12

Brown, J. W. (2005). *Process and the authentic life*. Heusenstamm: OntosVerlag.

Brown, J. W. (2010). Simultaneity and serial order. *Journal of Consciousness Studies*, *17*, 7–40.

Brown, J. W. (2011). *Gourmet's guide to the mind.* Belgium: Les éditions Chromatika.

Brown, J. W. (2012). *Love and other emotions: The process of feeling*. London: Karnac Books.

Brown, J. W. (2014). Feeling. *Journal of Mind and Behavior, 35*, 1–21.

Brown, J. W. (2015). *Microgenetic theory and process thought*. Exeter: Imprint Academic.

Brown, J. W. (2017). Microgenetic theory of memory, perception and the mental state: A brief review. *Journal of Consciousness Studies*, *24*, 51–70.

Brown, J. W. (2018). Simultaneity and serial order. In P. Stenner and M. Weber (Eds.), *Orpheus' Glance. Selected papers on process psychology: The Fontarèches meetings, 2002–2017*. Louvain-la-Neuve, Belgique: Les Editions Chromatika.

Brown, J. W. (2019). *Mental states and conceptual worlds*. Eugene, Oregon: Wipf and Stock.

Brown, J. W. (2020). Origins of subjective experience. *The Journal of Mind and Behavior.* Summer and autumn, *41*(3, 4), 267–276, ISSN 0271–0137.

Brown, J. W. (2021). The mind/brain state. *Journal of Mind and Behavior*, *42*, 1–16.

Brown, J. W. and Pachalska, M. (2003). The nature of the symptom and its relevance for neuropsychology. *Acta Neuropsychologica*, *1*(1), 1–11.

Brown, J. W. and Zhadiaiev, D. V. (2022). From drive to value. *Process Studies*, 1 November 2022; *51*(2), 204–220. https://doi.org/10.5406/21543682.51.2.04.

Changeux, P. (1985). *Neuronal man*. Oxford: Oxford University Press.

Deleuze, G. (1987). Lecture 12 o the Deleuze Seminars, available at Leibniz and the Baroque, Lecture 12, 10 March 1987 | The Deleuze Seminars. purdue.edu.

Dewey, J. (1939). *Theory of valuation*. Chicago, IL: University of Chicago Press.

Ebbeson, S. (1984). Evolution and ontogeny of neural circuits. *Behavioral and brain Sciences*, *7*, 321–366.

Faber, R. (2004). Whitehead at infinite speed: Deconstructing system as event. In C. Helmer (Ed.), *Schleiermacher and Whitehead open systems in dialogue* (pp. 39–72). Berlin, Boston: De Gruyter. https://doi.org/10.1515/9783110899658.39.

Franklin, G., Brown, J. W. and Freedman, M. (1982). Capgras syndrome a *deux*. *Lancet*, *2*, 222.

Freud, S. (1900). *The interpretation of dreams*. Standard edition. London: Hogarth Press.

Freud, S. (2010). *The interpretation of dreams*. J. Strachy (Ed.). New York: Basic Books (originally published 1955).

Gao, X., Wen, M., Sun, M. and Rossion, B. (2022). A genuine interindividual variability in number and anatomical localization of face-selective regions in the human brain. *Cereb Cortex*, *20*, *32*(21), 4834–4856. https://doi.org/10.1093/cercor/bhab519. PMID: 35088077.

Goodwin, B. (1982). Development and evolution. *Journal of Theoretical Biology*, *97*, 43–55.

Gould, S. (1982). *Ontogeny and phylogeny*. Cambridge, MA: Harvard University Press.

Graumann, C-F. (1959). Aktualgenese. *Zeitschrift für experimentelle und angewandte Psychologie*, *6*(3), 410–448.

Griffin, D. R. (2007). *Whitehead's radically different postmodern philosophy: An argument for its contemporary relevance*. New York: Albany.

Grober, E., Kellar, L., Perecman, E. and Brown, J. W. (1980). Lexical knowledge in anterior and posterior aphasics. *Brain and Language*, *10*, 313–330.

Hartmann, von E. (1931). *Philosophy of the unconscious* (Vol. 1–3). London: Kegan Paul. (Originally published 1868).

Heisenberg, W. (1958). *Physics and philosophy: The revolution in modern science*. London: Unwin University Books.

James, W. (1890). *The principles of psychology* (Vol. 1). New York: Henry Holt and Co.

James, W. (1911). *Some problems of philosophy*. London: Longmans Green and Co.

James, W. (1912/2003: 7). *Essays in radical empiricism*. New York: Dover.

James, W. (1890/1950). *The principles of psychology* (Vol. 1). New York: Dover.

Kelso, J., Holt, K., Kugler, P. and Turvey, M. (1980). On the concept of coordinative structures. In G. Stelmach and J. Requin (Eds.), *Tutorials in motor behavior* (pp. 1–47). Amsterdam: North-Holland. https://doi.org/10.1016/S0166-4115(08)61936-6.

Lashley, K. (1951). The problem of serial order in behavior. In L. Jeffress (Ed.), *Hixon symposium: Cerebral mechanisms in behavior* (pp.112–146). New York: Wiley.

Lavelli, M., Pantoja, A. P., Hsu, H., Messinger, D. and Fogel, A. (2005). Using microgenetic designs to study change processes. In D. M. Teti (Ed.), *Handbook of research methods in developmental science* (Vol. 4, pp. 40–65). Malden, MA: Blackwell. https://doi.org/10.1002/9780470756676.ch3.

Lestienne, R. (2022). *A. N. Whitehead – Philosopher of time*. London: World Scientific.

Libet, B. (1985). Unconscious cerebral initiative and the role of conscious will in voluntary activity. *Behavioral and Brain Science, 8*, 529–566.

Lindsley, D. (1951). Emotions. In S. Stevens (Ed.), *Handbook of experimenta psychology* (pp. 473–516). New York: Wiley.

Luria, A. (1969). *The mind of a mnemonist*. New York: Avon.

Lyotard, J-F. (1979). *The postmodern condition: A report on knowledge* (pp. 1–112). Manchester University Press.

MacLean, P. (1990). *The Triune brain in evolution*. New York: Plenum.

Mañjuśrī: Saptasatika: 213 in *The Perfection of wisdom in 700 lines*. Translated by Edward Conze. https://terebess.hu/english/Saptasatika.html.

McDowell, J. (1994). *Mind and world*. Cambridge, MA: Harvard University Press.

McTaggart, J. (1968). *Philosophical studies*. New York: Books for libraries (Originally published 1934).

Merleau–Ponty, M. (1962). *Phenomenology of perception*. London: Routledge.

Monakow, C. v. (1914). *Die Lokalisation im Grosshirn und der Abbau der Funktionen durch kortikale. Herde*. Wiesbaden: Bergmann.

Nagel, T. (2012). *Mind and cosmos*. Oxford: Oxford University Press.

O'Connor, T. (Ed. 1995). *Agents, causes, events*. Oxford: Oxford University Press.

Pachalska, M. (2012). Portrait of a scholar: Jason Walter Brown. Acta Neuropsychologica, *10*(1), 125–153.

Pachalska, M. and MacQueen, Bruce Duncan. (2005). Microgenetic theory: A new paradigm for contemporary neuropsychology and neurolinguistics. *Acta Neuropsychologica, 3*(3), 89–106.

Pears, D. (1963). *Freedom and the will*. London: MacMillan & Co.

Piaget, J, (1969). *The mechanisms of perception*. London: Routledge and Kegan Paul.

Poppel, E. (1988a). *Mindworks: Time and conscious experience*. San Diego, New York: Harcourt Brace Jovanovich.

Poppel, E. (1988b). Time perception. In *Sensory systems II-Senses other than vision (Encyclopedia of neuroscience)* (Vol. 2, pp. 134–135). Boston, MA: Birkhauser.

Salvatore, S. (2012). Social life of the sign: Sensemaking in society. In J. Valsiner (Ed.), *The Oxford handbook of culture and psychology* (pp. 241–254). Oxford: Oxford Press.

Schaefer, A., Kong, R. and Yeo, T. B. T. (2016). Functional connectivity parcellation of the human brain. In G. Wu, D. Shen, and M. Sabunen (Eds.), *Machine learning and medical imaging* (pp. 3–29). New York, San Diego, London, Oxford, Boston: Academic Press.

Schneirla, T. (1966). Behavioural development and comparative psychology. *Quarterly Reviews in Biology*, *41*, 283–302.

Seghal, M. (2016). *Eine situierte Metaphysik. Empirismus und Spekulation bei William James und Alfred North Whitehead.* Wallstein Verlag: Göttingen.

Semmes, J. (1968). Hemispheric specialization: A possible clue to mechanism. Neuropsychologia, *6*, 11–26.

Silberer, H. (1951). Report on a method of eliciting and observing certain hallucination phenomena. In D. Rapaport (Ed.), Organization and pathology of thought. New York: Columbia University Press.

Solms, M. (2000). Dreaming and REM sleep are controlled by different brain mechanisms. *Behavioral and Brain Sciences, 23*, 843–850.

Somel, M., Franz, H., Yan, Z., Lorenc, A., Guo, S., Giger, T., Kelso, J., Nickel, B., Dannemann, M., Bahn, S., Webster, M. J., Weickert, C. S., Lachmann, M., Paabo, S. and Khaitovich, P. (2009). Transcriptional neoteny in the human brain. *Proceedings of the National Academy of Sciences of the United States of America, 106*(14), 5743–5748.

Somel, M., Tang, L. and Khaitovich, P. (2012). *The role of neoteny in human evolution: From genes to the phenotype*. Tokyo: Springer. https://doi.org/10.1007/978-4-431-54011-3_3.

Sperry, R. (1980). Mind-brain interaction: Mentalism, yes; dualism, no. *Neuroscience, 5*, 195–206.

Stenner, P. (2011). James and Whitehead: Assemblage and systematization of a deeply empiricist mosaic philosophy. *European Journal of Pragmatism and American Philosophy*, *3*(1), 101–130.

Stenner, P. (2015). Emotion: Being moved beyond the mainstream. In Ian Parker (Ed.), *Handbook of critical psychology* (pp. 43–51). London: Routledge.

Stenner, P. (2017). *Liminality and experience: A transdisciplinarity approach to the psychosocial*. London: Palgrave.

Stenner, P. (2022). What is called "process thought": A transdisciplinary process ontology for psychosocial studies. In S. Frosh, M. Vyrgioti, and J. Walsh (Eds.), *The Palgrave handbook of psychosocial studies* (pp. 1–28). Palgrave Macmillan.

Stenner, P. and Andreouli, E. (2023). Revisioning psychology and deglobalisation: The case of brexit. *Theory & Psychology*, *33*(2), 209–226. https://doi.org/10.1177/09593543221135867

Stenner, P. and Nichterlein, M. (in press). We have always been postmodern: A new past for a future postmodern psychotherapy. In T. Strong and O. Smoliak (Eds.), *The Routledge international handbook of postmodern therapies*. London: Routledge.

Stroud, J. (1956). The fine structure of psychological time. In H. Quastler (Ed.), *Information theory in psychology* (pp. 174–205). IL: Free Press.

Toynbee, A. (1954). *A study of history* (Vol. 8). London, New York, Toronto: Oxford University Press.

Van Essen, D. C., Donahue, C. J., Coalson, T. S., Kennedy, H., Hayashi, T. and Glasser, M. F. (2019). Cerebral cortical folding, parcellation, and connectivity in humans, nonhuman primates, and mice. *Proceedings of the National academy of sciences of the United States of America. 116*(52), 26173–26180. [Advance online publication].

Varela, F. J. (1999). The specious present: A neurophenomenology of time consciousness. In J. Petitot, F. J. Varela, B. Pachoud, and J.- M. Roy (Eds.), Naturalizing *phenomenology* (pp. 266–314). Redwood City: Stanford University Press.

Vygotsky, L. S. (1962). *Thought and language*. Cambridge, MA: MIT Press.

Vygotsky, L. S. (1978). *Mind in society: The development of higher psychological processes*. Cambridge, MA: Harvard University Press.

Weizsaecker, V. von (1939/1958). *Le cycle de la structure*. Bruges: Desclee-De Brouwer.

Whitehead, A. N. (1917). *The organisation of thought.* London: Williams and Norgate, p. 141.

Whitehead, A. N. (1920). *The concept of nature*. Cambridge: Cambridge University Press.

Whitehead, A. N. (1924). Whitehead's first Harvard lecture, located at First Harvard Lecture. whiteheadresearch.org.

Whitehead, A. N. (1925/1985). *Science and the modern world.* London: Free Association Books.

Whitehead, A. N. (1926/1985). *Science and the modern world.* London: Free Association Books.

Whitehead, A. N. (1928/1985). *Process and reality*. New York: The Free Press.

Whitehead, A. N. (1933). *Adventures of ideas*. New York: Free Press.

Whitehead, A. N. (1934). *Nature and life*. Cambridge: Cambridge University Press.

Whitehead, A. N. (1938/1966). *Modes of thought*. New York: The Free Press.

Whitehead, A. N. (1978). *Process and reality.* New York: Free Press.

Yakovlev, P. (1948). Motility, behavior and the brain. *Journal of Nervous and Mental Disease*. *107*, 313–335.

Index

Note: *Italic* page numbers refer to figures and page numbers followed by "n" denote endnotes.

For Product Safety Concerns and Information please contact our EU representative GPSR@taylorandfrancis.com
Taylor & Francis Verlag GmbH, Kaufingerstraße 24, 80331 München, Germany

www.ingramcontent.com/pod-product-compliance
Lightning Source LLC
LaVergne TN
LVHW010925110826
845149LV00013B/2482

9781032879970